EXILES

JAMES JOYCE

Exiles

........By James Joyce

Edited By Pradip Das

For Reader

About Author

James Augustine[1] **Aloysius Joyce** (2 February 1882 – 13 January 1941) was an Irish novelist, short story writer, and poet. He contributed to the modernist avant-garde and is regarded as one of the most influential and important authors of the 20th century. Joyce is best known for *Ulysses* (1922), a landmark work in which the episodes of Homer's *Odyssey* are paralleled in a variety of literary styles, perhaps most prominently stream of consciousness. Other well-known works are the short-story collection *Dubliners* (1914), and the novels *A Portrait of the Artist as a Young Man* (1916) and *Finnegans Wake* (1939). His other writings include three books of poetry, a play, his published letters and occasional journalism.

About Editor

Pradip Das is a student and an 18 years old college going boy. He studies Geology at Jadavpur University. He is a passionate writer and Editor. He lives at West Bengal in India."Love, Ends with Blood" is his first story which is inspired by his friend's love life, and it is also available on Amazon Kindle.

Exiles
by James Joyce
RICHARD ROWAN, a writer.
BERTHA.
ARCHIE, their son, aged eight years.
ROBERT HAND, journalist.
BEATRICE JUSTICE, his cousin, music teacher.
BRIGID, an old servant of the Rowan family.
A FISHWOMAN.
At Merrion and Ranelagh, suburbs of Dublin.
Summer of the year 1912.
First Act
(The drawingroom in Richard Rowan's house at Merrion, a suburb of Dublin. On the right, forward, a
fireplace, before which stands a low screen. Over the mantelpiece a giltframed glass. Further back in the
right wall, folding doors leading to the parlour and kitchen. In the wall at the back to the right a small door
leading to a study. Left of this a sideboard. On the wall above the sideboard a framed crayon drawing of a

young man. More to the left double doors with glass panels leading out to the garden. In the wall at the left a
window looking out on the road. Forward in the same wall a door leading to the hall and the upper part of the
house. Between the window and door a lady's davenport stands against the wall. Near it a wicker chair. In the
centre of the room a round table. Chairs, upholstered in faded green plush, stand round the table. To the
right, forward, a smaller table with a smoking service on it. Near it an easychair and a lounge. Cocoanut
mats lie before the fireplace, beside the lounge and before the doors. The floor is of stained planking. The
double doors at the back and the folding doors at the right have lace curtains, which are drawn halfway. The
lower sash of the window is lifted and the window is hung with heavy green plush curtains. The blind is pulled

down to the edge of the lifted lower sash. It is a warm afternoon in June and the room is filled with soft
sunlight which is waning.)
(Brigid and Beatrice Justice come in by the door on the left. Brigid is an elderly woman, lowsized, with
irongrey hair. Beatrice Justice is a slender dark young woman of 27 years. She wears a wellmade navyblue
costume and an elegant simply trimmed black straw hat, and carries a small portfolioshaped handbag.)
BRIGID
The mistress and Master Archie is at the bath. They never expected you. Did you send word you were back,
Miss Justice?
BEATRICE
No. I arrived just now.
BRIGID
(Points to the easychair.) Sit down and I'll tell the master you are here. Were you long in the train?
BEATRICE
(Sitting down.) Since morning.
BRIGID
Master Archie got your postcard with the views of Youghal. You're tired out, I'm sure.
BEATRICE
O, no. *(She coughs rather nervously.)* Did he practise the piano while I was away?
BRIGID
(Laughs heartily.) Practice, how are you! Is it Master Archie? He is mad after the milkman's horse now. Had
you nice weather down there, Miss Justice?
BEATRICE
Rather wet, I think.
BRIGID
(Sympathetically.) Look at that now. And there is rain overhead too. *(Moving towards the study.)* I'll tell him

you are here.

BEATRICE
Is Mr Rowan in?
BRIGID
(Points.) He is in his study. He is wearing himself out about
something he is writing. Up half the night he does
be. *(Going.)* I'll call him.
BEATRICE
Don't disturb him, Brigid. I can wait here till they come back if they
are not long.
BRIGID
And I saw something in the letterbox when I was letting you in. *(She
crosses to the study door, opens it
slightly and calls.)* Master Richard, Miss Justice is here for Master
Archie's lesson.
*(Richard Rowan comes in from the study and advances towards
Beatrice, holding out his hand. He is a tall
athletic young man of a rather lazy carriage. He has light brown hair
and a moustache and wears glasses. He
is dressed in loose lightgrey tweed.)*
RICHARD
Welcome.
BEATRICE
(Rises and shakes hands, blushing slightly.) Good afternoon, Mr
Rowan. I did not want Brigid to disturb you.
RICHARD
Disturb me? My goodness!
BRIGID
There is something in the letterbox, sir.
RICHARD
(Takes a small bunch of keys from his pocket and hands them to her.)
Here.
*(Brigid goes out by the door at the left and is heard opening and
closing the box. A short pause. She enters
with two newspapers in her hands.)*
RICHARD
Letters?
BRIGID

No, sir. Only them Italian newspapers.
RICHARD
Leave them on my desk, will you?
*(Brigid hands him back the keys, leaves the newspapers in the study,
comes out again and goes out by the
folding doors on the right.)*
RICHARD
Please, sit down. Bertha will be back in a moment.
*(Beatrice sits down again in the easychair. Richard sits beside the
table.)*
RICHARD
I had begun to think you would never come back. It is twelve days
since you were here.
BEATRICE
I thought of that too. But I have come.
RICHARD
Have you thought over what I told you when you were here last?
BEATRICE
Very much.
RICHARD
You must have known it before. Did you? *(She does not answer.)* Do
you blame me?
BEATRICE
No.
RICHARD
Do you think I have acted towards you-- badly? No? Or towards
anyone?
BEATRICE
(Looks at him with a sad puzzled expression.) I have asked myself that
question.
RICHARD
And the answer?
BEATRICE
I could not answer it.
RICHARD

If I were a painter and told you I had a book of sketches of you you would not think it so strange, would you?

BEATRICE

It is not quite the same case, is it?

RICHARD

(Smiles slightly.) Not quite. I told you also that I would not show you what I had written unless you asked to see it. Well?

BEATRICE

I will not ask you.

RICHARD

(Leans forward, resting his elbows on his knees, his hands joined.) Would you like to see it?

BEATRICE

Very much.

RICHARD

Because it is about yourself?

BEATRICE

Yes. But not only that.

RICHARD

Because it is written by me? Yes? Even if what you would find there is sometimes cruel?

BEATRICE

(Shyly.) That is part of your mind, too.

RICHARD

Then it is my mind that attracts you? Is that it?

BEATRICE

(Hesitating, glances at him for an instant.) Why do you think I come here?

RICHARD

Why? Many reasons. To give Archie lessons. We have known one another so many years, from childhood, Robert, you and I-- haven't we? You have always been interested in me, before I went away and while I was away. Then our letters to each other about my book. Now it is published. I am here again. Perhaps you feel

that some new thing is gathering in my brain; perhaps you feel that you should know it. Is that the reason?
BEATRICE
No.
RICHARD
Why, then?
BEATRICE
Otherwise I could not see you.
(She looks at him for a moment and then turns aside quickly.)
RICHARD
(After a pause repeats uncertainly.) Otherwise you could not see me?
BEATRICE
(Suddenly confused.) I had better go. They are not coming back. *(Rising.)* Mr Rowan, I must go.
RICHARD
(Extending his arms.) But you are running away. Remain. Tell me what your words mean. Are you afraid of
me?
BEATRICE
(Sinks back again.) Afraid? No.
RICHARD
Have you confidence in me? Do you feel that you know me?
BEATRICE
(Again shyly.) It is hard to know anyone but oneself.
RICHARD
Hard to know me? I sent you from Rome the chapters of my book as I wrote them; and letters for nine long
years. Well, eight years.
BEATRICE
Yes, it was nearly a year before your first letter came.

RICHARD
It was answered at once by you. And from that on you have watched me in my struggle. *(Joins his hands
earnestly.)* Tell me, Miss Justice, did you feel that what you read was written for your eyes? Or that you
inspired me?

BEATRICE
(Shakes her head.) I need not answer that question.
RICHARD
What then?
BEATRICE
(Is silent for a moment.) I cannot say it. You yourself must ask me, Mr Rowan.
RICHARD
(With some vehemence.) Then that I expressed in those chapters and letters, and in my character and life as
well, something in your soul which you could not-- pride or scorn?
BEATRICE
Could not?
RICHARD
(Leans towards her.) Could not because you dared not. Is that why?
BEATRICE
(Bends her head.) Yes.
RICHARD
On account of others or for want of courage-- which?
BEATRICE
(Softly.) Courage.
RICHARD
(Slowly.) And so you have followed me with pride and scorn also in your heart?
BEATRICE
And loneliness.
(She leans her head on her hand, averting her face. Richard rises and walks slowly to the window on the left.

He looks out for some moments and then returns towards her, crosses to the lounge and sits down near her.)
RICHARD
Do you love him still?
BEATRICE
I do not even know.
RICHARD

It was that that made me so reserved with you-- then-- even though I felt your interest in me, even though I
felt that I too was something in your life.

BEATRICE

You were.

RICHARD

Yet that separated me from you. I was a third person I felt. Your names were always spoken together, Robert
and Beatrice, as long as I can remember. It seemed to me, to everyone...

BEATRICE

We are first cousins. It is not strange that we were often together.

RICHARD

He told me of your secret engagement with him. He had no secrets from me; I suppose you know that.

BEATRICE

(Uneasily.) What happened-- between us-- is so long ago. I was a child.

RICHARD

(Smiles maliciously.) A child? Are you sure? It was in the garden of his mother's house. No? *(He points
towards the garden.)* Over there. You plighted your troth, as they say, with a kiss. And you gave him your
garter. Is it allowed to mention that?

BEATRICE

(With some reserve.) If you think it worthy of mention.

RICHARD

I think you have not forgotten it. *(Clasping his hands quietly.)* I do not understand it. I thought, too, that after I
had gone... Did my going make you suffer?

BEATRICE

I always knew you would go some day. I did not suffer; only I was changed.

RICHARD

Towards him?

BEATRICE

Everything was changed. His life, his mind, even, seemed to change after that.

RICHARD

(Musing.) Yes. I saw that you had changed when I received your first letter after a year; after your illness, too.
You even said so in your letter.

BEATRICE

It brought me near to death. It made me see things differently.

RICHARD

And so a coldness began between you, little by little. Is that it?

BEATRICE

(Half closing her eyes.) No. Not at once. I saw in him a pale reflection of you: then that too faded. Of what
good is it to talk now?

RICHARD

(With a repressed energy.) But what is this that seems to hang over you? It cannot be so tragic.

BEATRICE

(Calmly.) O, not in the least tragic. I shall become gradually better, they tell me, as I grow older. As I did not
die then they tell me I shall probably live. I am given life and health again-- when I cannot use them. *(Calmly
and bitterly.)* I am convalescent.

RICHARD

(Gently.) Does nothing then in life give you peace? Surely it exists for you somewhere.

BEATRICE

If there were convents in our religion perhaps there. At least, I think so at times.

RICHARD

(Shakes his head.) No, Miss Justice, not even there. You could not give yourself freely and wholly.

BEATRICE

(Looking at him.) I would try.

RICHARD

You would try, yes. You were drawn to him as your mind was drawn towards mine. You held back from him.

From me, too, in a different way. You cannot give yourself freely and wholly.

BEATRICE

(Joins her hands softly.) It is a terribly hard thing to do, Mr Rowan-- to give oneself freely and wholly-- and

be happy.

RICHARD

But do you feel that happiness is the best, the highest that we can know?

BEATRICE

(With fervour.) I wish I could feel it.

RICHARD

(Leans back, his hands locked together behind his head.) O, if you knew how I am suffering at this moment!

For your case, too. But suffering most of all for my own. *(With bitter force.)* And how I pray that I may be

granted again my dead mother's hardness of heart! For some help, within me or without, I must find. And find

it I will.

(Beatrice rises, looks at him intently, and walks away toward the garden door. She turns with indecision,

looks again at him and, coming back, leans over the easychair.)

BEATRICE

(Quietly.) Did she send for you before she died, Mr Rowan?

RICHARD

(Lost in thought.) Who?

BEATRICE

Your mother.

RICHARD

(Recovering himself, looks keenly at her for a moment.) So that, too, was said of me here by my friends-- that

she sent for me before she died and that I did not go?

BEATRICE

Yes.

RICHARD

(Coldly.) She did not. She died alone, not having forgiven me, and fortified by the rites of holy church.

BEATRICE

Mr Rowan, why did you speak to me in such a way?

RICHARD

(Rises and walks nervously to and fro.) And what I suffer at this moment you will say is my punishment.

BEATRICE

Did she write to you? I mean before...

RICHARD

(Halting.) Yes. A letter of warning, bidding me break with the past, and remember her last words to me.

BEATRICE

(Softly.) And does death not move you, Mr Rowan? It is an end. Everything else is so uncertain.

RICHARD

While she lived she turned aside from me and from mine. That is certain.

BEATRICE

From you and from...?

RICHARD

From Bertha and from me and from our child. And so I waited for the end as you say; and it came.

BEATRICE

(Covers her face with her hands.) O, no. Surely no.

RICHARD

(Fiercely.) How can my words hurt her poor body that rots in the grave? Do you think I do not pity her cold
blighted love for me? I fought against her spirit while she lived to the bitter end. *(He presses his hand to his
forehead.)* It fights against me still-- in here.

BEATRICE

(As before.) O, do not speak like that.

RICHARD

She drove me away. On account of her I lived years in exile and poverty too, or near it. I never accepted the doles she sent me through the bank. I waited, too, not for her death but for some understanding of me, her own

son, her own flesh and blood; that never came.

BEATRICE

Not even after Archie...?

RICHARD

(Rudely.) My son, you think? A child of sin and shame! Are you serious? *(She raises her face and looks at him.)* There were tongues here ready to tell her all, to embitter her withering mind still more against me and Bertha and our godless nameless child. *(Holding out his hands to her.)* Can you not hear her mocking me while I speak? You must know the voice, surely, the voice that called you *the black protestant,* the pervert's daughter. *(With sudden selfcontrol.)* In any case a remarkable woman.

BEATRICE

(Weakly.) At least you are free now.

RICHARD

(Nods.) Yes, she could not alter the terms of my father's will nor live for ever.

BEATRICE

(With joined hands.) They are both gone now, Mr Rowan. They both loved you, believe me. Their last thoughts were of you.

RICHARD

(Approaching, touches her lightly on the shoulder, and points to the crayon drawing on the wall.) Do you see him there, smiling and handsome? His last thoughts! I remember the night he died. *(He pauses for an instant and then goes on calmly.)* I was a boy of fourteen. He called me to his bedside. He knew I wanted to go to the theater to hear *Carmen.* He told my mother to give me a shilling. I kissed him and went. When I came home he was dead. Those were his last thoughts as far as I know.

BEATRICE

The hardness of heart you prayed for... *(She breaks off.)*

RICHARD

(Unheeding.) That is my last memory of him. Is there not something sweet and noble in it?

BEATRICE

Mr Rowan, something is on your mind to make you speak like this. Something has changed you since you came back three months ago.

RICHARD

(Gazing again at the drawing, calmly, almost gaily.) He will help me, perhaps, my smiling handsome father.

(A knock is heard at the hall door on the left.)

RICHARD

(Suddenly.) No, no. Not the smiler, Miss Justice. The old mother. It is her spirit I need. I am going.

BEATRICE

Someone knocked. They have come back.

RICHARD

No, Bertha has a key. It is he. At least, I am going, whoever it is. *(He goes out quickly on the left and comes back at once with his straw hat in his hand.)*

BEATRICE

He? Who?

RICHARD

O, probably Robert. I am going out through the garden. I cannot see him now. Say I have gone to the post. Goodbye.

BEATRICE

(With growing alarm.) It is Robert you do not wish to see?

RICHARD

(Quietly.) For the moment, yes. This talk has upset me. Ask him to wait.

BEATRICE

You will come back?

RICHARD

Please God.

(He goes out quickly through the garden. Beatrice makes as if to follow him. and then stops after a few paces.
Brigid enters by the folding doors on the right and goes out on the left. The hall door is heard opening. A few
seconds after Brigid enters with Robert Hand. Robert Hand is a middlesized, rather stout man between thirty
and forty. He is cleanshaven, with mobile features. His hair and eyes are dark and his complexion sallow. His
gait and speech are rather slow. He wears a dark blue morning suit and carries in his hand a large bunch of
red roses wrapped in tissue paper.)

ROBERT

(Coming toward. her with outstretched hand which she takes.) My dearest coz. Brigid told me you were here.
I had no notion. Did you send mother a telegram?

BEATRICE

(Gazing at the roses.) No.

ROBERT

(Following her gaze.) You are admiring my roses. I brought them to the mistress of the house. *(Critically.)* I
am afraid they are not nice.

BRIGID

O, they are lovely, sir. The mistress will be delighted with them.

ROBERT

(Lays the roses carelessly on a chair out of sight.) Is nobody in?

BRIGID

Yes, sir. Sit down, sir. They'll be here now any moment. The master was here. *(She looks about her and with a*
half curtsey goes out on the right.)

ROBERT

(After a short silence.) How are you, Beatty? And how are all down in Youghal? As dull as ever?

BEATRICE

They were well when I left.

ROBERT

(Politely.) O, but I'm sorry I did not know you were coming. I would have met you at the train. Why did you
do it? You have some queer ways about you, Beatty, haven't you?
BEATRICE
(In the same tone.) Thank you, Robert. I am quite used to getting about alone.
ROBERT
Yes, but I mean to say... O, well, you have arrived in your own characteristic way. *(A noise is heard at the
window and a boy's voice is heard calling,* Mr Hand! *Robert turns.)*
By Jove, Archie, too, is arriving in a
characteristic way!
*(Archie scrambles into the room through the open window on the left and then rises to his feet, flushed and
panting. Archie is a boy of eight years, dressed in white breeches, jersey and cap. He wears spectacles, has a
lively manner and speaks with the slight trace of a foreign accent.)*
BEATRICE
(Going towards him.) Goodness gracious, Archie! What is the matter?

ARCHIE
(Rising, out of breath.) Eh! I ran all the avenue.
ROBERT
(Smiles and holds out his hand.) Good evening, Archie. Why did you run?
ARCHIE
(Shakes hands.) Good evening. We saw you on the top of the tram, and I shouted *Mr Hand!* But you did not
see me. But we saw you, mamma and I. She will be here in a minute. I ran.
BEATRICE
(Holding out her hand.) And poor me!
ARCHIE
(Shakes hands somewhat shyly.) Good evening, Miss Justice.
BEATRICE
Were you disappointed that I did not come last Friday for the lesson?
ARCHIE

(Glancing at her, smiles.) No.
BEATRICE
Glad?
ARCHIE
(Suddenly.) But today it is too late.
BEATRICE
A very short lesson?
ARCHIE
(Pleased.) Yes.
BEATRICE
But now you must study, Archie.
ROBERT
Were you at the bath?

ARCHIE
Yes.
ROBERT
Are you a good swimmer now?
ARCHIE
(Leans against the davenport.) No. Mamma won't let me into the deep place. Can you swim well, Mr Hand?
ROBERT
Splendidly. Like a stone.
ARCHIE
(Laughs.) Like a stone! *(Pointing down.)* Down that way?
ROBERT
(Pointing.) Yes, down; straight down. How do you say that over in Italy?
ARCHIE
That? *Giù. (Pointing down and up.)* That is *giù* and this is *sù*. Do you want to speak to my pappie?
ROBERT
Yes. I came to see him.
ARCHIE
(Going towards the study) I will tell him. He is in there, writing.
BEATRICE

(Calmly, looking at Robert.) No; he is out. He is gone to the post with some letters.

ROBERT

(Lightly.) O, never mind. I will wait if he is only gone to the post.

ARCHIE

But mamma is coming. *(He glances towards the window.)* Here she is!

(Archie runs out by the door on the left. Beatrice walks slowly towards the davenport. Robert remains standing. A short silence. Archie and Bertha come in through the door on the left. Bertha is a young woman of graceful build. She has dark grey eyes, patient in expression, and soft features. Her manner is cordial and selfpossessed. She wears a lavender dress and carries her cream gloves knotted round the handle of her sunshade.)

BERTHA

(Shaking hands.) Good evening, Miss Justice. We thought you were still down in Youghal.

BEATRICE

(Shaking hands.) Good evening, Mrs Rowan.

BERTHA

(Bows.) Good evening, Mr Hand.

ROBERT

(Bowing.) Good evening, *signora!* Just imagine, I didn't know either she was back till I found her here.

BERTHA

(To both.) Did you not come together?

BEATRICE

No. I came first. Mr Rowan was going out. He said you would be back any moment.

BERTHA

I'm sorry. If you had written or sent over word by the girl this morning...

BEATRICE

(Laughs nervously.) I arrived only an hour and a half ago. I thought of sending a telegram but it seemed too
tragic.
BERTHA
Ah? Only now you arrived?
ROBERT
(Extending his arms, blandly.) I retire from public and private life. Her first cousin and a journalist, I know
nothing of her movements.
BEATRICE
(Not directly to him.) My movements are not very interesting.
ROBERT
(In the same tone.) A lady's movements are always interesting.

BERTHA
But sit down, won't you? You must be very tired.
BEATRICE
(Quickly.) No, not at all. I just came for Archie's lesson.
BERTHA
I wouldn't hear of such a thing, Miss Justice, after your long journey.
ARCHIE
(Suddenly to Beatrice.) And, besides, you didn't bring the music.
BEATRICE
(A little confused.) That I forgot. But we have the old piece.
ROBERT
(Pinching Archie's ear.) You little scamp. You want to get off the lesson.
BERTHA
O, never mind the lesson. You must sit down and have a cup of tea now. *(Going towards the door on the
right.)* I'll tell Brigid.
ARCHIE
I will, mamma. *(He makes a movement to go.)*
BEATRICE
No, please Mrs Rowan. Archie! I would really prefer...
ROBERT
(Quietly.) I suggest a compromise. Let it be a half-lesson.

BERTHA
But she must be exhausted.
BEATRICE
(Quickly.) Not in the least. I was thinking of the lesson in the train.
ROBERT
(To Bertha.) You see what it is to have a conscience, Mrs Rowan.

ARCHIE
Of my lesson, Miss Justice?
BEATRICE
(Simply.) It is ten days since I heard the sound of a piano.
BERTHA
O, very well. If that is it...
ROBERT
(Nervously, gaily.) Let us have the piano by all means. I know what is in Beatty's ears at this moment. *(To Beatrice.)* Shall I tell?
BEATRICE
If you know.
ROBERT
The buzz of the harmonium in her father's parlour. *(To Beatrice.)* Confess.
BEATRICE
(Smiling.) Yes. I can hear it.
ROBERT
(Grimly.) So can I. The asthmatic voice of protestantism.
BERTHA
Did you not enjoy yourself down there, Miss Justice?
ROBERT
(Intervenes.) She did not, Mrs Rowan. She goes there on retreat, when the protestant strain in her prevails--
gloom, seriousness, righteousness.
BEATRICE
I go to see my father.
ROBERT
(Continuing.) But she comes back here to my mother, you see. The piano influence is from our side of the

house.
BERTHA

(Hesitating.) Well, Miss Justice, if you would like to play
something... But please don't fatigue yourself with
Archie.
ROBERT
(Suavely.) Do, Beatty. That is what you want.
BEATRICE
If Archie will come?
ARCHIE
(With a shrug.) To listen.
BEATRICE
(Takes his hand.) And a little lesson, too. Very short.
BERTHA
Well, afterwards you must stay to tea.
BEATRICE
(To Archie.) Come.
*(Beatrice and Archie go out together by the door on the left. Bertha
goes towards the davenport, takes off her
hat and lays it with her sunshade on the desk. Then taking a key from
a little flowervase, she opens a drawer
of the davenport, takes out a slip of paper and closes the drawer
again. Robert stands watching her.)*
BERTHA
(Coming towards him with the paper in her hand.) You put this into
my hand last night. What does it mean?
ROBERT
Do you not know?
BERTHA
(Reads.) There is one word which I have never dared to say to you.
What is the word?
ROBERT
That I have a deep liking for you.
(A short pause. The piano is heard faintly from the upper room.)
ROBERT

(Takes the bunch of roses from the chair.) I brought these for you.
Will you take them from me?

BERTHA
(Taking them.) Thank you. *(She lays them on the table and unfolds the paper again.)* Why did you not dare to
say it last night?
ROBERT
I could not speak to you or follow you. There were too many people
on the lawn. I wanted you to think over it
and so I put it into your hand when you were going away.
BERTHA
Now you have dared to say it.
ROBERT
(Moves his hand slowly past his eyes.) You passed. The avenue was
dim with dusky light. I could see the dark
green masses of the trees. And you passed beyond them. You were
like the moon.
BERTHA
(Laughs.) Why like the moon?
ROBERT
In that dress, with your slim body, walking with little even steps. I
saw the moon passing in the dusk till you
passed and left my sight.
BERTHA
Did you think of me last night?
ROBERT
(Comes nearer.) I think of you always-- as something beautiful and
distant-- the moon or some deep music.
BERTHA
(Smiling.) And last night which was I?
ROBERT
I was awake half the night. I could hear your voice. I could see your
face in the dark. Your eyes... I want to
speak to you. Will you listen to me? May I speak?
BERTHA
(Sitting down.) You may.

ROBERT
(Sitting beside her.) Are you annoyed with me?

BERTHA
No.
ROBERT
I thought you were. You put away my poor flowers so quickly.
BERTHA
(Takes them from the table and holds them close to her face.) Is this
what you wish me to do with them?
ROBERT
(Watching her.) Your face is a flower too-- but more beautiful. A wild
flower blowing in a hedge. *(Moving his
chair closer to her.)* Why are you smiling? At my words?
BERTHA
(Laying the flowers in her lap.) I am wondering if that is what you
say-- to the others.
ROBERT
(Surprised.) What others?
BERTHA
The other women. I hear you have so many admirers.
ROBERT
(Involuntarily.) And that is why you too...?
BERTHA
But you have, haven't you?
ROBERT
Friends, yes.
BERTHA
Do you speak to them in the same way?
ROBERT
(In an offended tone.) How can you ask me such a question? What
kind of person do you think I am? Or why
do you listen to me? Did you not like me to speak to you in that way?
BERTHA

What you said was very kind. *(She looks at him for a moment.)* Thank you for saying it-- and thinking it.

ROBERT

(Leaning forward.) Bertha!

BERTHA

Yes?

ROBERT

I have the right to call you by your name. From old times-- nine years ago. We were Bertha-- and Robert--
then. Can we not be so now, too?

BERTHA

(Readily.) O yes. Why should we not?

ROBERT

Bertha, you knew. From the very night you landed on Kingstown pier. It all came back to me then. And you
knew it. You saw it.

BERTHA

No. Not that night.

ROBERT

When?

BERTHA

The night we landed I felt very tired and dirty. *(Shaking her head.)* I did not see it in you that night.

ROBERT

(Smiling.) Tell me what did you see that night-- your very first impression.

BERTHA

(Knitting her brows.) You were standing with your back to the gangway, talking to two ladies.

ROBERT

To two plain middleaged ladies, yes.

BERTHA

I recognized you at once. And I saw that you had got fat.

ROBERT

(Takes her hand.) And this poor fat Robert-- do you dislike him then so much? Do you disbelieve all he says?

BERTHA
I think men speak like that to all women whom they like or admire.
What do you want me to believe?
ROBERT
All men, Bertha?
BERTHA
(With sudden sadness.) I think so.
ROBERT
I too?
BERTHA
Yes, Robert. I think you too.
ROBERT
All then-- without exception? Or with one exception? *(In a lower
tone.)* Or is he too-- Richard too-- like us
all-- in that at least? Or different?
BERTHA
(Looks into his eyes.) Different.
ROBERT
Are you quite sure, Bertha?
BERTHA
(A little confused, tries to withdraw her hand.) I have answered you.
ROBERT
(Suddenly.) Bertha, may I kiss your hand? Let me. May I?
BERTHA
If you wish.
(He lifts her hand to his lips slowly. She rises suddenly. and listens.)
BERTHA

Did you hear the garden gate?
ROBERT
(Rising also.) No.
(A short pause. The piano can be heard faintly from the upper room.)
ROBERT
(Pleading.) Do not go away. You must never go away now. Your life
is here. I came for that too today-- to
speak to him-- to urge him to accept this position. He must. And you
must persuade him to. You have a great

influence over him.

BERTHA

You want him to remain here.

ROBERT

Yes.

BERTHA

Why?

ROBERT

For your sake because you are unhappy so far away. For his sake too because he should think of his future.

BERTHA

(Laughing.) Do you remember what he said when you spoke to him last night?

ROBERT

About...? *(Reflecting.)* Yes. He quoted the *Our Father* about our daily bread. He said that to take care for the
future is to destroy hope and love in the world.

BERTHA

Do you not think he is strange?

ROBERT

In that, yes.

BERTHA

A little-- mad?

ROBERT

(Comes closer.) No. He is not. Perhaps we are. Why, do you...?

BERTHA

(Laughs.) I ask you because you are intelligent.

ROBERT

You must not go away. I will not let you.

BERTHA

(Looks full at him.) You?

ROBERT

Those eyes must not go away. *(He takes her hands.)* May I kiss your eyes?

BERTHA

Do so. *(He kisses her eyes and then passes his hand over her hair.)*

ROBERT
Little Bertha!
BERTHA
(Smiling.) But I am not so little. Why do you call me little?
ROBERT
Little Bertha! One embrace? *(He puts his arm around her.)* Look into my eyes again.
BERTHA
(Looks.) I can see the little gold spots. So many you have.
ROBERT
(Delighted.) Your voice! Give me a kiss, a kiss with your mouth.
BERTHA
Take it.
ROBERT
I am afraid. *(He kisses her mouth and passes his hand many times over her hair.)* At last I hold you in my
arms!
BERTHA

And are you satisfied?
ROBERT
Let me feel your lips touch mine.
BERTHA
And then you will be satisfied?
ROBERT
(Murmurs.) Your lips, Bertha!
BERTHA
(Closes her eyes and kisses him quickly.) There. *(Puts her hands on his shoulders.)* Why don't you say:
thanks?
ROBERT
(Sighs.) My life is finished-- over.
BERTHA
O, don't speak like that now, Robert.
ROBERT
Over, over. I want to end it and have done with it.
BERTHA

(Concerned but lightly.) You silly fellow!
ROBERT
(Presses her to him.) To end it all-- death. To fall from a great high cliff, down, right down into the sea.
BERTHA
Please, Robert...
ROBERT
Listening to music and in the arms of the woman I love-- the sea, music and death.
BERTHA
(Looks at him for a moment.) The woman you love?
ROBERT

(Hurriedly.) I want to speak to you, Bertha-- alone-- not here. Will you come?
BERTHA
(With downcast eyes.) I too want to speak to you.
ROBERT
(Tenderly.) Yes, dear, I know. *(He kisses her again.)* I will speak to you; tell you all; then. I will kiss you,
then, long long kisses-- when you come to me-- long long sweet kisses.
BERTHA
Where?
ROBERT
(In tone of passion.) Your eyes. Your lips. All your divine body.
BERTHA
(Repelling his embrace, confused.) I meant where do you wish me to come.
ROBERT
To my house. Not my mother's over there. 1 will write the address for you. Will you come?
BERTHA
When?
ROBERT
Tonight. Between eight and nine. Come. I will wait for you tonight. And every night. You will?

(He kisses her with passion, holding her head between his hands.
After a few instants she breaks from him. He
sits down.)
BERTHA
(Listening.) The gate opened.
ROBERT
(Intensely.) I will wait for you.
(He takes the slip from the table. Bertha moves away from him slowly.
Richard comes in from the garden.)
RICHARD
(Advancing, takes off his hat.) Good afternoon.

ROBERT
(Rises, with nervous friendliness.) Good afternoon, Richard.
BERTHA
(At the table, taking the roses.) Look what lovely roses Mr Hand
brought me.
ROBERT
I am afraid they are overblown.
RICHARD
(Suddenly.) Excuse me for a moment, will you?
(He turns and goes into his study quickly. Robert takes a pencil from
his pocket and writes a few words on the
slip; then hands it quickly to Bertha.)
ROBERT
(Rapidly.) The address. Take the tram at Lansdowne Road and ask to
be let down near there.
BERTHA
(Takes it.) I promise nothing.
ROBERT
I will wait.
(Richard comes back from the study.)
BERTHA
(Going.) I must put these roses in water.
RICHARD
(Handing her his hat.) Yes, do. And please put my hat on the rack.
BERTHA

(Takes it.) So I will leave you to yourselves for your talk. *(Looking round.)* Do you want anything?
Cigarettes?
RICHARD
Thanks. We have them here.
BERTHA

Then I can go?
(She goes out on the left with Richard's hat, which she leaves in the hall, and returns at once; she stops for a
moment at the davenport, replaces the slip do the drawer, locks it, and replaces the key, and, taking the roses,
goes towards the right. Robert precedes her to open the door for her. She bows and goes out.)
RICHARD
(Points to the chair near the little table on the right.) Your place of honour.
ROBERT
(Sits down.) Thanks. *(Passing his hand over his brow.)* Good Lord, how warm it is today! The heat pains me
here in the eye. The glare.
RICHARD
The room is rather dark, I think, with the blind down but if you wish...
ROBERT
(Quickly.) Not at all. I know what it is-- the result of night work.
RICHARD
(Sits on the lounge.) Must you?
ROBERT
(Sighs.) Eh, yes. I must see part of the paper through every night. And then my leading articles. We are
approaching a difficult moment. And not only here.
RICHARD
(After a slight pause.) Have you any news?
ROBERT
(In a different voice.) Yes. I want to speak to you seriously. Today may be an important day for you-- or

rather, tonight. I saw the vicechancellor this morning. He has the highest opinion of you, Richard. He has read your book, he said.

RICHARD

Did he buy it or borrow it?

ROBERT

Bought it, I hope.

RICHARD

I shall smoke a cigarette. Thirty-seven copies have now been sold in Dublin. *(He takes a cigarette from the box on the table, and lights it.)*

ROBERT

(Suavely, hopelessly.) Well, the matter is closed for the present. You have your iron mask on today.

RICHARD

(Smoking.) Let me hear the rest.

ROBERT

(Again seriously.) Richard, you are too suspicious. It is a defect in you. He assured me he has the highest possible opinion of you, as everyone has. You are the man for the post, he says. In fact, he told me that, if your name goes forward, he will work might and main for you with the senate and I... will do my part, of course, in the press and privately. I regard it as a public duty. The chair of romance literature is yours by right, as a scholar, as a literary personality.

RICHARD

The conditions?

ROBERT

Conditions? You mean about the future?

RICHARD

I mean about the past.

ROBERT

(Easily.) That episode in your past is forgotten. An act of impulse. We are all impulsive

RICHARD

(Looks fixedly at him.) You called it an act of folly, then-- nine years ago. You told me I was hanging a weight
about my neck.
ROBERT
I was wrong. *(Suavely.)* Here is how the matter stands, Richard.
Everyone knows that you ran away years ago
with a young girl... How shall I put it? ...with a young girl not exactly your equal. *(Kindly.)* Excuse me,
Richard, that is not my opinion nor my language. I am simply using the language of people whose opinions I
don't share.
RICHARD
Writing one of your leading articles, in fact.
ROBERT

Put it so. Well, it made a great sensation at the time. A mysterious disappearance. My name was involved too,
as best man, let us say, on that famous occasion. Of course, they think I acted from a mistaken sense of
friendship. Well, all that is known. *(With some hesitation.)* But what happened afterwards is not known.
RICHARD
No?
ROBERT
Of course, it is your affair, Richard. However, you are not so young now as you were then. The expression is
quite in the style of my leading articles, isn't it?
RICHARD
Do you, or do you not, want me to give the lie to my past life?
ROBERT
I am thinking of your future life-- here. I understand your pride and your sense of liberty. I understand their
point of view also. However, there is a way out; it is simply this. Refrain from contradicting any rumours you
may hear concerning what happened.... or did not happen after you went away. Leave the rest to me.
RICHARD

You will set these rumours afloat?
ROBERT
I will. God help me.
RICHARD
(Observing him.) For the sake of social conventions?
ROBERT
For the sake of something else too-- our friendship, our lifelong friendship.
RICHARD
Thanks.
ROBERT
(Slightly wounded.) And I will tell you the whole truth.
RICHARD
(Smiles and bows.) Yes. Do, please.
ROBERT

Not only for your sake. Also for the sake of-- your present partner in life.
RICHARD
I see.
(He crushes his cigarette softly on the ashtray and then leans forward, rubbing his hands slowly.)
RICHARD
Why for her sake?
ROBERT
(Also leans forward, quietly.) Richard, have you been quite fair to her? It was her own free choice, you will
say. But was she really free to choose? She was a mere girl. She accepted all that you proposed.
RICHARD
(Smiles.) That is your way of saying that she proposed what I would not accept.
ROBERT
(Nods.) I remember. And she went away with you. But was it of her own free choice? Answer me frankly.
RICHARD

(Turns to him, calmly.) I played for her against all that you say or can say; and I won.
ROBERT
(Nodding again.) Yes, you won.
RICHARD
(Rises.) Excuse me for forgetting. Will you have some whisky?
ROBERT
All things come to those who wait.
*(Richard goes to the sideboard and brings a small tray with the decanter and glasses to the table where he
sets it down.)*
RICHARD
(Sits down again, leaning back on the lounge.) Will you please help yourself?
ROBERT
(Does so.) And you? Steadfast? *(Richard shakes his head.)* Lord, when I think of our wild nights long ago--
talks by the hour, plans, carouses, revelry...

RICHARD
In our house.
ROBERT
It is mine now. I have kept it ever since though I don't go there often. Whenever you like to come let me
know. You must come some night. It will be old times again. *(He lifts his glass, and drinks.)* Prosit!
RICHARD
It was not only a house of revelry; it was to be the hearth of a new life. *(Musing.)* And in that name all our sins
were committed.
ROBERT
Sins! Drinking and blasphemy *(he points)* by me. And drinking and heresy, much worse *(he points again)* by
you-- are those the sins you mean?
RICHARD
And some others.
ROBERT

(Lightly, uneasily.) You mean the women. I have no remorse of conscience. Maybe you have. We had two keys on those occasions. *(Maliciously.)* Have you?

RICHARD

(Irritated.) For you it was all quite natural?

ROBERT

For me it is quite natural to kiss a woman whom I like. Why not? She is beautiful for me.

RICHARD

(Toying with the lounge cushion.) Do you kiss everything that is beautiful for you?

ROBERT

Everything-- if it can be kissed. *(He takes up a flat stone which lies on the table.)* This stone, for instance. It is so cool, so polished, so delicate, like a woman's temple. It is silent, it suffers our passion; and it is beautiful.
(He places it against his lips.) And so I kiss it because it is beautiful. And what is a woman? A work of nature, too, like a stone or a flower or a bird. A kiss is an act of homage.

RICHARD

It is an act of union between man and woman. Even if we are often led to desire through the sense of beauty can you say that the beautiful is what we desire?

ROBERT

(Pressing the stone to his forehead.) You will give me a headache if you make me think today. I cannot think today. I feel too natural, too common. After all, what is most attractive in even the most beautiful woman?

RICHARD

What?

ROBERT

Not those qualities which she has and other women have not but the qualities which she has in common with them. I mean... the commonest. *(Turning over the stone, he presses the other side to his forehead.)* I mean

how her body develops heat when it is pressed, the movement of her blood, how quickly she changes by
digestion what she eats into-- what shall be nameless. *(Laughing.)* I am very common today. Perhaps that idea
never struck you?

RICHARD

(Drily.) Many ideas strike a man who has lived nine years with a woman.

ROBERT

Yes. I suppose they do.... This beautiful cool stone does me good. Is it a paperweight or a cure for headache?

RICHARD

Bertha brought it home one day from the strand. She, too, says that it is beautiful.

ROBERT

(Lays down the stone quietly.) She is right.
(He raises his glass, and drinks. A pause.)

RICHARD

Is that all you wanted to say to me?

ROBERT

(Quickly.) There is something else. The vicechancellor sends you, through me, an invitation for tonight-- to
dinner at his house. You know where he lives? *(Richard nods.)* I thought you might have forgotten. Strictly
private, of course. He wants to meet you again and sends you a very warm invitation.

RICHARD

For what hour?

ROBERT

Eight. But, like yourself, he is free and easy about time. Now, Richard, you must go there. That is all. I feel

tonight will be the turningpoint in your life. You will live here and work here and think here and be honoured
here-- among our people.

RICHARD

(Smiling.) I can almost see two envoys starting for the United States to collect funds for my statue a hundred
years hence.
ROBERT
(Agreeably.) Once I made a little epigram about statues. All statues are of two kinds. *(He folds his arms
across his chest.)* The statue which says: *How shall I get down?* and the other kind *(he unfolds his arms and
extends his right arm, averting his head)* the statue which says: *In my time the dunghill was so high.*
RICHARD
The second one for me, please.
ROBERT
(Lazily.) Will you give me one of those long cigars of yours?
(Richard selects a Virginia cigar from the box on the table and hands it to him with the straw drawn out.)
ROBERT
(Lighting it.) These cigars Europeanize me. If Ireland is to become a new Ireland she must first become
European. And that is what you are here for, Richard. Some day we shall have to choose between England and
Europe. I am a descendant of the dark foreigners: that is why I like to be here. I may be childish. But where
else in Dublin can I get a bandit cigar like this or a cup of black coffee? The man who drinks black coffee is
going to conquer Ireland. And now I will take just a half measure of that whisky, Richard, to show you there
is no ill feeling.
RICHARD
(Points.) Help yourself.
ROBERT
(Does so.) Thanks. *(He drinks and goes on as before.)* Then you yourself, the way you loll on that lounge:
then your boy's voice and also-- Bertha herself. Do you allow me to call her that, Richard? I mean as an old
friend of both of you.
RICHARD

O, why not?
ROBERT
(With animation.) You have that fierce indignation which lacerated
the heart of Swift. You have fallen from a
higher world, Richard, and you are filled with fierce indignation,
when you find that life is cowardly and
ignoble. While I... shall I tell you?

RICHARD
By all means.
ROBERT
(Archly.) I have come up from a lower world and I am filled with
astonishment when I find that people have
any redeeming virtue at all.
RICHARD
(Sits up suddenly and leans his elbows on the table.) You are my
friend, then?
ROBERT
(Gravely.) I fought for you all the time you were away. I fought to
bring you back. I fought to keep your place
for you here. I will fight for you still because I have faith in you, the
faith of a disciple in his master. I cannot
say more than that. It may seem strange to you... Give me a match.
RICHARD
(Lights and offers him a match.) There is a faith still stranger than the
faith of the disciple in his master.
ROBERT
And that is?
RICHARD
The faith of a master in the disciple who will betray him.
ROBERT
The church lost a theologian in you, Richard. But I think you look too
deeply into life. *(He rises, pressing*
Richard's arm slightly.) Be gay. Life is not worth it.
RICHARD
(Without rising.) Are you going?
ROBERT

Must. *(He turns and says in a friendly tone.)* Then it is all arranged.
We meet tonight at the vicechancellor's. I
shall look in at about ten. So you can have an hour or so to yourselves
first. You will wait till I come?
RICHARD
Good.
ROBERT
One more match and I am happy.

(Richard strikes another match, hands it to him and rises also. Archie comes in by the door on the left,
followed by Beatrice.)
ROBERT
Congratulate me, Beatty. I have won over Richard.
ARCHIE
(Crossing to the door on the right, calls.) Mamma, Miss Justice is
going.
BEATRICE
On what are you to be congratulated?
ROBERT
On a victory, of course. *(Laying his hand lightly on Richard's*
shoulder.) The descendant of Archibald
Hamilton Rowan has come home.
RICHARD
I am not a descendant of Hamilton Rowan.
ROBERT
What matter? *(Bertha comes in from the right with a bowl of roses.)*
BEATRICE
Has Mr Rowan...?
ROBERT
(Turning towards Bertha.) Richard is coming tonight to the
vicechancellor's dinner. The fatted calf will be
eaten: roast, I hope. And next session will see the descendant of a
namesake of etcetera, etcetera in a chair of
the university. *(He offers his hand.)* Good afternoon, Richard. We
shall meet tonight.
RICHARD

(Touches his hand.) At Philippi.
BEATRICE
(Shakes hands also.) Accept my best wishes, Mr Rowan.
RICHARD
Thanks. But do not believe him.
ROBERT

(Vivaciously.) Believe me, believe me. *(To Bertha.)* Good afternoon, Mrs Rowan.
BERTHA
(Shaking hands, candidly.) I thank you, too. *(To Beatrice.)* You won't stay to tea, Miss Justice?
BEATRICE
No, thank you. *(Takes leave of her.)* I must go. Good afternoon. Goodbye, Archie *(going).*
ROBERT
Addio, Archibald.
ARCHIE
Addio.
ROBERT
Wait, Beatty. I shall accompany you.
BEATRICE
(Going out on the right with Bertha.) O, don't trouble.
ROBERT
(Following her.) But I insist-- as a cousin.
(Bertha, Beatrice and Robert go out by the door on the left. Richard stands irresolutely near the table. Archie closes the door leading to the hall and, coming over to him, plucks him by the sleeve.)
ARCHIE
I say, pappie!
RICHARD
(Absently.) What is it?
ARCHIE
I want to ask you a thing.
RICHARD
(Sitting on the end of the lounge, stares in front of him.) What is it?

ARCHIE
Will you ask mamma to let me go out in the morning with the
milkman?

RICHARD
With the milkman?
ARCHIE
Yes. In the milkcar. He says he will let me drive when we get on to
the roads where there are no people. The
horse is a very good beast. Can I go?
RICHARD
Yes.
ARCHIE
Ask mamma now can I go. Will you?
RICHARD
(Glances towards the door.) I will.
ARCHIE
He said he will show me the cows he has in the field. Do you know
how many cows he has?
RICHARD
How many?
ARCHIE
Eleven. Eight red and three white. But one is sick now. No, not sick.
But it fell.
RICHARD
Cows?
ARCHIE
(With a gesture.) Eh! Not bulls. Because bulls give no milk. Eleven
cows. They must give a lot of milk. What
makes a cow give milk?
RICHARD
(Takes his hand.) Who knows? Do you understand what it is to give a
thing?
ARCHIE
To give? Yes.
RICHARD

While you have a thing it can be taken from you.
ARCHIE
By robbers? No?
RICHARD
But when you give it, you have given it. No robber can take it from you. *(He bends his head and presses his son's hand against his cheek.)* It is yours then for ever when you have given it. It will be yours always. That is to give.
ARCHIE
But, pappie?
RICHARD
Yes?
ARCHIE
How could a robber rob a cow? Everyone would see him. In the night, perhaps.
RICHARD
In the night, yes.
ARCHIE
Are there robbers here like in Rome?
RICHARD
There are poor people everywhere.
ARCHIE
Have they revolvers?
RICHARD
No.
ARCHIE
Knives? Have they knives?
RICHARD
(Sternly.) Yes, yes. Knives and revolvers.

ARCHIE
(Disengages himself.) Ask mamma now. She is coming.
RICHARD
(Makes a movement to rise.) I will.
ARCHIE

No, sit there, pappie. You wait and ask her when she comes back. I won't be here. I'll be in the garden.
RICHARD
(Sinking back again.) Yes. Go.
ARCHIE
(Kisses him swiftly.) Thanks.
(He runs out quickly by the door at the back leading into the garden. Bertha enters by the door on the left. She
approaches the table and stands beside it, fingering the petals of the roses, looking at Richard.)
RICHARD
(Watching her.) Well?
BERTHA
(Absently.) Well. He says he likes me.
RICHARD
(Leans his chin in his hand.) You showed him his note?
BERTHA
Yes. I asked him what it meant.
RICHARD
What did he say it meant?
BERTHA
He said I must know. I said I had an idea. Then he told me he liked me very much. That I was beautiful-- and
all that.
RICHARD
Since when!

BERTHA
(Again absently.) Since when-- what?
RICHARD
Since when did he say he liked you?
BERTHA
Always, he said. But more since we came back. He said I was like the moon in this lavender dress. (Looking
at him.) Had you any words with him-- about me?
RICHARD
(Blandly.) The usual thing. Not about you.

BERTHA
He was very nervous. You saw that?
RICHARD
Yes. I saw it. What else went on?
BERTHA
He asked me to give him my hand.
RICHARD
(Smiling.) In marriage?
BERTHA
(Smiling.) No, only to hold.
RICHARD
Did you?
BERTHA
Yes. *(Tearing off a few petals.)* Then he caressed my hand and asked
would I let him kiss it. I let him.
RICHARD
Well?
BERTHA
Then he asked could he embrace me-- even once? ..and then...

RICHARD
And then?
BERTHA
He put his arm round me.
RICHARD
(Stares at the floor for a moment, then looks at her again.) And then?
BERTHA
He said I had beautiful eyes. And asked could he kiss them. *(With a
gesture.)* I said: *Do so.*
RICHARD
And he did?
BERTHA
Yes. First one and then the other. *(She breaks off suddenly.)* Tell me,
Dick, does all this disturb you? Because
I told you I don't want that. I think you are only pretending you don't
mind. I don't mind.
RICHARD

(Quietly.) I know, dear. But I want to find out what he means or feels just as you do.

BERTHA

(Points at him.) Remember, you allowed me to go on. I told you the whole thing from the beginning.

RICHARD

(As before.) I know, dear... And then?

BERTHA

He asked for a kiss. I said: *Take it.*

RICHARD

And then?

BERTHA

(Crumpling a handful of petals.) He kissed me.

RICHARD

Your mouth?

BERTHA

Once or twice.

RICHARD

Long kisses?

BERTHA

Fairly long. *(Reflects.)* Yes, the last time.

RICHARD

(Rubs his hands slowly; then:) With his lips? Or... the other way?

BERTHA

Yes, the last time.

RICHARD

Did he ask you to kiss him?

BERTHA

He did.

RICHARD

Did you?

BERTHA

(Hesitates, then looking straight at him.) I did. I kissed him.

RICHARD

What way?

BERTHA

(With a shrug.) O simply.
RICHARD
Were you excited?
BERTHA
Well, you can imagine. *(Frowning suddenly.)* Not much. He has not
nice lips... Still I was excited, of course.
But not like with you, Dick.

RICHARD
Was he?
BERTHA
Excited? Yes, I think he was. He sighed. He was dreadfully nervous.
RICHARD
(Resting his forehead on his hand.) I see.
BERTHA
(Crosses towards the lounge and stands near him.) Are you jealous?
RICHARD
(As before.) No.
BERTHA
(Quietly.) You are, Dick.
RICHARD
I am not. Jealous of what?
BERTHA
Because he kissed me.
RICHARD
(Looks up.) Is that all?
BERTHA
Yes, that's all. Except that he asked me would I meet him.
RICHARD
Out somewhere?
BERTHA
No. In his house.
RICHARD
(Surprised.) Over there with his mother, is it?

BERTHA

No, a house he has. He wrote the address for me.
(She goes to the desk, takes the key from the flower vase, unlocks the drawer and returns to him with the slip
of paper.)
RICHARD
(Half to himself.) Our cottage.
BERTHA
(Hands him the slip.) Here.
RICHARD
(Reads it.) Yes. Our cottage.
BERTHA
Your...?
RICHARD
No, his. I call it ours. *(Looking at her.)* The cottage I told you about so often-- that we had the two keys for, he
and I. It is his now. Where we used to hold our wild nights, talking, drinking, planning-- at that time. Wild
nights; yes. He and I together. *(He throws the slip on the couch and rises suddenly.)* And sometimes I alone.
(Stares at her.) But not quite alone. I told you. You remember?
BERTHA
(Shocked.) That place?
RICHARD
(Walks away from her a few paces and stands still, thinking, holding his chin.) Yes.
BERTHA
(Taking up the slip again.) Where is it?
RICHARD
Do you not know?
BERTHA
He told me to take the tram at Lansdowne Road and to ask the man to let me down there. Is it... is it a bad
place?
RICHARD

O no, cottages. *(He returns to the lounge and sits down.)* What answer did you give?

BERTHA
No answer. He said he would wait.
RICHARD
Tonight?
BERTHA
Every night, he said. Between eight and nine.
RICHARD
And so I am to go tonight to interview-- the professor. About the appointment I am to beg for. *(Looking at her.)* The interview is arranged for tonight by him-- between eight and nine. Curious, isn't it? The same hour.
BERTHA
Very.
RICHARD
Did he ask you had I any suspicion?
BERTHA
No.
RICHARD
Did he mention my name?
BERTHA
No.
RICHARD
Not once?
BERTHA
Not that I remember.
RICHARD
(Bounding to his feet.) O yes! Quite clear!
BERTHA

What?
RICHARD
(Striding to and fro.) A liar, a thief, and a fool! Quite clear! A common thief! What else? *(With a harsh laugh.)* My great friend! A patriot too! A thief-- nothing else! *(He halts, thrusting his hands into his pockets.)* But a fool also!
BERTHA

(Looking at him.) What are you going to do?
RICHARD
(Shortly.) Follow him. Find him. Tell him. *(Calmly.)* A few words
will do. Thief and fool.
BERTHA
(Flings the slip on the couch.) I see it all!
RICHARD
(Turning.) Eh!
BERTHA
(Hotly.) The work of a devil.
RICHARD
He?
BERTHA
(Turning on him.) No, you! The work of a devil to turn him against
me as you tried to turn my own child
against me. Only you did not succeed.
RICHARD
How? In God's name, how?
BERTHA
(Excitedly.) Yes, yes. What I say. Everyone saw it. Whenever I tried
to correct him for the least thing you
went on with your folly, speaking to him as if he were a grownup
man. Ruining the poor child, or trying to.
Then, of course, I was the cruel mother and only you loved him. *(With
growing excitement.)* But you did not
turn him against me-- against his own mother. Because why? Because
the child has too much nature in him.
RICHARD
I never tried to do such a thing, Bertha. You know I cannot be severe
with a child.

BERTHA
Because you never loved your own mother. A mother is always a
mother, no matter what. I never heard of any
human being that did not love the mother that brought him into the
world, except you.
RICHARD

(Approaching her quietly.) Bertha, do not say things you will be sorry for. Are you not glad my son is fond of
me?

BERTHA

Who taught him to be? Who taught him to run to meet you? Who told him you would bring him home toys
when you were out on your rambles in the rain, forgetting all about him-- and me? I did. I taught him to love
you.

RICHARD

Yes, dear. I know it was you.

BERTHA

(Almost crying.) And then you try to turn everyone against me. All is to be for you. I am to appear false and
cruel to everyone except to you. Because you take advantage of my simplicity as you did-- the first time.

RICHARD

(Violently.) And you have the courage to say that to me?

BERTHA

(Facing him.) Yes, I have! Both then and now. Because I am simple you think you can do what you like with
me. *(Gesticulating.)* Follow him now. Call him names. Make him be humble before you and make him
despise me. Follow him!

RICHARD

(Controlling himself.) You forget that I have allowed you complete liberty-- and allow you it still.

BERTHA

(Scornfully.) Liberty!

RICHARD

Yes, complete. But he must know that I know. *(More calmly.)* I will speak to him quietly. *(Appealing.)*
Bertha, believe me, dear! It is not jealousy. You have complete liberty to do as you wish-- you and he. But not
in this way. He will not despise you. You don't wish to deceive me or to pretend to deceive me-- with him, do
you?

BERTHA

No, I do not. *(Looking full at him.)* Which of us two is the deceiver?
RICHARD
Of us? You and me?
BERTHA
(In a calm decided tone.) I know why you have allowed me what you call complete liberty.
RICHARD
Why?
BERTHA
To have complete liberty with-- that girl.
RICHARD
(Irritated.) But, good God, you knew about that this long time. I never hid it.
BERTHA
You did. I thought it was a kind of friendship between you-- till we came back, and then I saw.
RICHARD
So it is, Bertha.
BERTHA
(Shakes her head.) No, no. It is much more; and that is why you give me complete liberty. All those things
you sit up at night to write about *(pointing to the study)* in there-- about her. You call that friendship?
RICHARD
Believe me, Bertha dear. Believe me as I believe you.
BERTHA
(With an impulsive gesture) My God, I feel it! I know it! What else is between you but love?
RICHARD
(Calmly.) You are trying to put that idea into my head but I warn you that I don't take my ideas from other
people.
BERTHA
(Hotly.) It is, it is! And that is why you allow him to go on. Of course! It doesn't affect you. You love her.

RICHARD
Love! *(Throws out his hands with a sigh and moves away from her.)* I cannot argue with you.
BERTHA
You can't because I am right. *(Following him a few steps.)* What would anyone say?
RICHARD
(Turns to her.) Do you think I care?
BERTHA
But I care. What would he say if he knew? You, who talk so much of the high kind of feeling you have for
me, expressing yourself in that way to another woman. If he did it, or other men, I could understand because
they are all false pretenders. But you, Dick! Why do you not tell him then?
RICHARD
You can if you like.
BERTHA
I will. Certainly I will.
RICHARD
(Coolly.) He will explain it to you.
BERTHA
He doesn't say one thing and do another. He is honest in his own way.
RICHARD
(Plucks one of the roses and throws it at her feet.) He is, indeed! The soul of honour!
BERTHA
You may make fun of him as much as you like. I understand more than you think about that business. And so
will he. Writing those long letters to her for years, and she to you. For years. But since I came back I
understand it-- well.
RICHARD
You do not. Nor would he.
BERTHA

(Laughs scornfully.) Of course. Neither he nor I can understand it.
Only she can. Because it is such a deep
thing!

RICHARD
(Angrily.) Neither he nor you-- nor she either! Not one of you!
BERTHA
(With great bitterness.) She will! She will understand it! The diseased
woman!
*(She turns away and walks over to the little table on the right.
Richard restrains a sudden gesture. A short
pause.)*
RICHARD
(Gravely.) Bertha, take care of uttering words like that!
BERTHA
(Turning, excitedly.) I don't mean any harm! I feel for her more than
you can because I am a woman. I do,
sincerely. But what I say is true.
RICHARD
Is it generous? Think.
BERTHA
(Pointing towards the garden.) It is she who is not generous.
Remember now what I say.
RICHARD
What?
BERTHA
(Comes nearer; in a calmer tone.) You have given that woman very
much, Dick. And she may be worthy of
it. And she may understand it all, too. I know she is that kind.
RICHARD
Do you believe that?
BERTHA
I do. But I believe you will get very little from her in return-- or from
any of her clan. Remember my words,
Dick. Because she is not generous and they are not generous. Is it all
wrong what I am saying? Is it?
RICHARD

(Darkly.) No. Not all.
(She stoops and, picking up the rose from the floor, places it in the vase again. He watches her. Brigid
appears at the folding doors on the right.)

BRIGID
The tea is on the table, ma'am.
BERTHA
Very well.
BRIGID
Is Master Archie in the garden?
BERTHA
Yes. Call him in.
(Brigid crosses the room and goes out into the garden. Bertha goes towards the doors on the right. At the
lounge she stops and takes up the slip.)
BRIGID
(In the garden.) Master Archie! You are to come in to your tea.
BERTHA
Am I to go to this place?
RICHARD
Do you want to go?
BERTHA
I want to find out what he means. Am I to go?
RICHARD
Why do you ask me? Decide yourself.
BERTHA
Do you tell me to go?
RICHARD
No.
BERTHA
Do you forbid me to go?
RICHARD

No.
BRIGID

(From the garden.) Come quickly, Master Archie! Your tea is waiting on you.
(Brigis crosses the room and goes out through the folding doors. Bertha folds the slip into the waist of her
dress and goes slowly towards the right. Near the door she turns and halts.)
BERTHA
Tell me not to go and I will not.
RICHARD
(Without looking at her.) Decide yourself.
BERTHA
Will you blame me then?
RICHARD
(Excitedly.) No, no! I will not blame you. You are free. I cannot blame you.
(Archie appears at the garden door.)
BERTHA
I did not deceive you. *(She goes out through the folding doors. Richard remains standing at the table. Archie, when his mother has gone, runs down to Richard.)*
ARCHIE
(Quickly.) Well, did you ask her?
RICHARD
(Starting.) What?
ARCHIE
Can I go?
RICHARD
Yes.
ARCHIE
In the morning? She said yes?

RICHARD
Yes. In the morning.
(He puts his arm round his son's shoulders and looks down at him fondly.)
Second Act

(A room in Robert Hand's cottage at Ranelagh. On the right, forward, a small black piano, on the rest of
which is an open piece of music. Farther back a door leading to the street door. In the wall, at the back,
folding doors, draped with dark curtains, leading to a bedroom. Near the piano a large table, on which is a
tall oil lamp with a wide yellow shade. Chairs, upholstered, near this table. A small cardtable more forward.
Against the back wall a bookcase. In the left wall, back, a window looking out into the garden, and, forward,
a door and porch, also leading to the garden. Easychairs here and there. Plants in the porch and near the
draped folding doors. On the walls are many framed black and white designs. In the right corner, back, a
sideboard; and in the centre of the room, left of the table, a group consisting of a standing Turkish pipe, a low
oil stove, which is not lit, and a rocking chair. It is the evening of the same day.)
(Robert Hand, in evening dress, is seated at the piano. The candles are not lit but the lamp on the table is lit.
He plays softly in the bass the first bars of Wolfram's song in the last act of Tannhäuser. *Then he breaks off*
and, resting an elbow on the ledge of the keyboard, meditates. Then he rises and, pulling out a pump from
behind the piano, walks here and there in the room ejecting from it into the air sprays of perfume. He inhales
the air slowly and then puts the pump buck behind the piano. He sits down on a chair near the table and,
smoothing his hair carefully, sighs once or twice. Then, thrusting his hands into his trousers pockets, he leans
back, stretches out his legs, and waits. A knock is heard at the street door. He rises quickly.)
ROBERT
(Exclaims.) Bertha!
(He hurries out by the door on the right. There is a noise of confused greeting. After a few moments Robert

enters, followed by Richard Rowan, who is in gray tweeds as before
but holds in one hand a dark felt hat and
in the other an umbrella.)
ROBERT
First of all let me put these outside. *(He takes the hat and umbrella,*
leaves them in the hall and returns.)
ROBERT
(Pulling round a chair.) Here you are. You are lucky to find me in.
Why didn't you tell me today? You were
always a devil for surprises. I suppose my evocation of the past was
too much for your wild blood. See how
artistic I have become. *(He points to the walls.)* The piano is an
addition since your time. I was just strumming
out Wagner when you came. Killing time. You see I am ready for the
fray. *(Laughs.)* I was just wondering
how you and the vicechancellor were getting on together. *(With*
exaggerated alarm.) But are you going in that
suit? O well, it doesn't make much odds, I suppose. But how goes the
time? *(He takes out his watch.)* Twenty
past eight already, I declare!
RICHARD

Have you an appointment?
ROBERT
(Laughs nervously.) Suspicious to the last!
RICHARD
Then I may sit down?
ROBERT
Of course, of course. *(They both sit down.)* For a few minutes,
anyhow. Then we can both go on together. We
are not bound for time. Between eight and nine, he said, didn't he?
What time is it, I wonder? *(Is about to look*
again at his watch; then stops.) Twenty past eight, yes.
RICHARD
(Wearily, sadly.) Your appointment also was for the same hour. Here.
ROBERT
What appointment?

RICHARD
With Bertha.
ROBERT
(Stares at him.) Are you mad?
RICHARD
Are you?
ROBERT
(After a long pause.) Who told you?
RICHARD
She.
(A short silence.)
ROBERT
(In a low voice.) Yes. I must have been mad. *(Rapidly.)* Listen to me, Richard. It is a great relief to me that
you have come-- the greatest relief. I assure you that ever since this afternoon I have thought and thought how
I could break it off without seeming a fool. A great relief! I even intended to send word... a letter, a few lines.
(Suddenly.) But then it was too late... *(Passes his hand over his forehead.)* Let me speak frankly with you; let

me tell you everything.
RICHARD
I know everything. I have known for some time.
ROBERT
Since when?
RICHARD
Since it began between you and her.
ROBERT
(Again rapidly.) Yes, I was mad. But it was merely lightheadedness. I admit that to have asked her here this
evening was a mistake. I can explain everything to you. And I will. Truly.
RICHARD
Explain to me what is the word you longed and never dared to say to her. If you can or will.
ROBERT

(Looks down, then raises his head.) Yes. I will. I admire very much the personality of your... of... your wife.
That is the word. I can say it. It is no secret.
RICHARD
Then why did you wish to keep secret your wooing?
ROBERT
Wooing?
RICHARD
Your advances to her, little by little, day after day, looks, whispers. *(With a nervous movement of the hands.)*
Insomma, wooing.
ROBERT
(Bewildered.) But how do you know all this?
RICHARD
She told me.
ROBERT
This afternoon?

RICHARD
No. Time after time, as it happened.
ROBERT
You knew? From her? *(Richard nods.)*. You were watching us all the time?
RICHARD
(Very coldly.) I was watching you.
ROBERT
(Quickly.) I mean, watching me. And you never spoke! You had only to speak a word-- to save me from
myself. You were trying me. *(Passes his hand again over his forehead.)* It was a terrible trial: now also.
(Desperately.) Well, it is past. It will be a lesson to me for all my life. You hate me now for what I have done
and for...
RICHARD
(Quietly, looking at him.) Have I said that I hate you?
ROBERT
Do you not? You must.

RICHARD
Even if Bertha had not told me I should have known. Did you not see that when I came in this afternoon I
went into my study suddenly for a moment?
ROBERT
You did. I remember.
RICHARD
To give you time to recover yourself. It made me sad to see your eyes. And the roses too. I cannot say why. A
great mass of overblown roses.
ROBERT
I thought I had to give them. Was that strange? *(Looks at Richard with a tortured expression.)* Too many,
perhaps? Or too old or common?
RICHARD
That was why I did not hate you. The whole thing made me sad all at once.
ROBERT

(To himself.) And this is real. It is happening-- to us.
(He stares before him for some moments in silence, as if dazed; then, without turning his head, continues.)
ROBERT
And she, too, was trying me; making an experiment with me for your sake!
RICHARD
You know women better than I do. She says she felt pity for you.
ROBERT
(Brooding.) Pitied me, because I am no longer... an ideal lover. Like my roses. Common, old.
RICHARD
Like all men you have a foolish wandering heart.
ROBERT
(Slowly.) Well, you spoke at last. You chose the right moment.
RICHARD
(Leans forward.) Robert, not like this. For us two, no. Years, a whole life, of friendship. Think a moment.

Since childhood, boyhood... No, no. Not in such a way-- like thieves--
at night. *(Glancing about him.)* And in
such a place. No, Robert, that is not for people like us.
ROBERT
What a lesson! Richard, I cannot tell you what a relief it is to me that
you have spoken-- that the danger is
passed. Yes, yes. *(Somewhat diffidently.)* Because... there was some
danger for you, too, if you think. Was
there not?
RICHARD
What danger?
ROBERT
(In the same tone.) I don't know. I mean if you had not spoken. If you
had watched and waited on until...
RICHARD
Until?
ROBERT
(Bravely.) Until I had come to like her more and more (because I can
assure you it is only a lightheaded idea
of mine), to like her deeply, to love her. Would you have spoken to
me then as you have just now? *(Richard is*

silent. Robert goes on more boldly.) It would have been different,
would it not? For then it might have been
too late while it is not too late now. What could I have said then? I
could have said only: You are my friend,
my dear good friend. I am very sorry but I love her. *(With a sudden
fervent gesture.)* I love her and I will take
her from you, however I can, because I love her.
(They look at each other for some moments in silence.)
RICHARD
(Calmly.) That is the language I have heard often and never believed
in. Do you mean by stealth or by
violence? Steal you could not in my house because the doors were
open: nor take by violence if there were no
resistance.
ROBERT

You forget that the kingdom of heaven suffers violence: and the kingdom of heaven is like a woman.

RICHARD

(Smiling.) Go on.

ROBERT

(Diffidently, but bravely.) Do you think you have rights over her-- over her heart?

RICHARD

None.

ROBERT

For what you have done for her? So much! You claim nothing?

RICHARD

Nothing.

ROBERT

(After a pause strikes his forehead with his hand.) What am I saying? Or what am I thinking? I wish you would upbraid me, curse me, hate me as I deserve. You love this woman. I remember all you told me long ago. She is yours, your work. *(Suddenly.)* And that is why I, too, was drawn to her. You are so strong that you attract me even through her.

RICHARD

I am weak.

ROBERT

(With enthusiasm.) You, Richard! You are the incarnation of strength.

RICHARD

(Holds out his hands.) Feel those hands.

ROBERT

(Taking his hands.) Yes. Mine are stronger. But I meant strength of another kind.

RICHARD

(Gloomily.) I think you would try to take her by violence. *(He withdraws his hands slowly.)*

ROBERT

(Rapidly.) Those are moments of sheer madness when we feel an intense passion for a woman. We see

nothing. We think of nothing. Only to possess her. Call it brutal, bestial, what you will.
RICHARD
(A little timidly.) I am afraid that that longing to possess a woman is not love.
ROBERT
(Impatiently.) No man ever yet lived on thus earth who did not long to possess-- I mean to possess in the
flesh-- the woman whom he loves. It is nature's law.
RICHARD
(Contemptuously.) What is that to me? Did I vote it?
ROBERT
But if you love... What else is it?
RICHARD
(Hesitatingly.) To wish her well.
ROBERT
(Warmly.) But the passion which burns us night and day to possess her. You feel it as I do. And it is not what
you said now.
RICHARD
Have you...? *(He stops for an instance.)* Have you the luminous certitude that yours is the brain in contact
with which she must think and understand and that yours is the body in contact with which her body must
feel? Have you this certitude in yourself?
ROBERT
Have you?

RICHARD
(Moved.) Once I had it, Robert: a certitude as luminous as that of my own existence-- or an illusion as
luminous.
ROBERT
(Cautiously.) And now?
RICHARD
If you had it and I could feel that you had it-- even now...
ROBERT

What would you do?

RICHARD

(Quietly.) Go away. You, and not I, would be necessary to her. Alone as I was before I met her.

ROBERT

(Rubs his hands nervously.) A nice little load on my conscience!

RICHARD

(Abstractedly.) You met my son when you came to my house this afternoon. He told me. What did you feel?

ROBERT

(Promptly.) Pleasure.

RICHARD

Nothing else?

ROBERT

Nothing else. Unless I thought of two things at the same time. I am like that. If my best friend lay in his coffin and his face had a comic expression I should smile. *(With a little gesture of despair.)* I am like that. But I should suffer too, deeply.

RICHARD

You spoke of conscience... Did he seem to you a child only-- or an angel?

ROBERT

(Shakes his head.) No. Neither an angel nor an Anglo-Saxon. Two things, by the way, for which I have very little sympathy.

RICHARD

Never then? Never even... with her? Tell me. I wish to know.

ROBERT

I feel in my heart something different. I believe that on the last day (if it ever comes), when we are all assembled together, that the Almighty will speak to us like this. We will say that we lived chastely with one other creature...

RICHARD

(Bitterly.) Lie to Him?

ROBERT

Or that we tried to. And He will say to us: Fools! Who told you that you were to give yourselves to one being

only? You were made to give yourselves to many freely. I wrote that law with My finger on your hearts.

RICHARD

On woman's heart, too?

ROBERT

Yes. Can we close our heart against an affection which we feel deeply? Should we close it? Should she?

RICHARD

We are speaking of bodily union.

ROBERT

Affection between man and woman must come to that. We think too much of it because our minds are

warped. For us today it is of no more consequence than any other form of contact-- than a kiss.

RICHARD

If it is of no consequence why are you dissatisfied till you reach that end? Why were you waiting here

tonight?

ROBERT

Passion tends to go as far as it can; but, you may believe me or not, I had not that in my mind-- to reach that

end.

RICHARD

Reach it if you can. I will use no arm against you that the world puts in my hand. If the law which God's

finger has written on our hearts is the law you say I too am God's creature.

(He rises and paces to and fro some moments in silence. Then he goes towards the porch and leans against

the jamb. Robert watches him.)

ROBERT

I always felt it. In myself and in others.

RICHARD

(Absently.) Yes?
ROBERT
(With a vague gesture.) For all. That a woman, too, has the right to try with many men until she finds love. An
immoral idea, is it not? I wanted to write a book about it. I began it...
RICHARD
(As before.) Yes?
ROBERT
Because I knew a woman who seemed to me to be doing that-- carrying out that idea in her own life. She
interested me very much.
RICHARD
When was this?
ROBERT
O, not lately. When you were away.
(Richard leaves his place rather abruptly and again paces to and fro.)
ROBERT
You see, I am more honest than you thought.
RICHARD
I wish you had not thought of her now-- whoever she was, or is.
ROBERT
(Easily.) She was and is the wife of a stockbroker.
RICHARD
(Turning.) You know him?
ROBERT

Intimately.
(Richard sits down again in the same place and leans forward, his head on his hands.)
ROBERT
(Moving his chair a little closer.) May I ask you a question?
RICHARD
You may.
ROBERT
(With some hesitation.) Has it never happened to you in these years-- I mean when you were away from her,

perhaps, or travelling-- to... betray her with another. Betray her, I mean, not in love. Carnally, I mean... Has
that never happened?
RICHARD
It has.
ROBERT
And what did you do?
RICHARD
(As before.) I remember the first time. I came home. It was night. My house was silent. My little son was
sleeping in his cot. She, too, was asleep. I wakened her from sleep and told her. I cried beside her bed; and I
pierced her heart.
ROBERT
O, Richard, why did you do that?
RICHARD
Betray her?
ROBERT
No. But tell her, waken her from sleep to tell her. It was piercing her heart.
RICHARD
She must know me as I am.
ROBERT
But that is not you as you are. A moment of weakness.

RICHARD
(Lost in thought.) And I was feeding the flame of her innocence with my guilt.
ROBERT
(Brusquely.) O, don't talk of guilt and innocence. You have made her all that she is. A strange and wonderful
personality-- in my eyes, at least.
RICHARD
(Darkly.) Or I have killed her.
ROBERT
Killed her?
RICHARD

The virginity of her soul.

ROBERT

(Impatiently.) Well lost! What would she be without you?

RICHARD

I tried to give her a new life.

ROBERT

And you have. A new and rich life.

RICHARD

Is it worth what I have taken from her-- her girlhood, her laughter, her young beauty, the hopes in her young
heart?

ROBERT

(Firmly.) Yes. Well worth it. *(He looks at Richard for some moments in silence.)* If you had neglected her,
lived wildly, brought her away so far only to make her suffer...
(He stops. Richard raises his head, and looks at him.)

RICHARD

If I had?

ROBERT

(Slightly confused.) You know there were rumours here of your life abroad-- a wild life. Some persons who

knew you or met you or heard of you in Rome. Lying rumours.

RICHARD

(Coldly.) Continue.

ROBERT

(Laughs a little harshly.) Even I at times thought of her as a victim. *(Smoothly.)* And of course, Richard, I felt
and knew all the time that you were a man of great talent-- of something more than talent. And that was your
excuse-- a valid one in my eyes.

RICHARD

Have you thought that it is perhaps now-- at this moment-- that I am neglecting her? *(He clasps his hands
nervously and leans across toward Robert.)* I may be silent still. And she may yield to you at last-- wholly and
many times.

ROBERT
(Draws back at once.) My dear Richard, my dear friend, I swear to you I could not make you suffer.

RICHARD
(Continuing.) You may then know in soul and body, in a hundred forms, and ever restlessly, what some old
theologian, Duns Scotus, I think, called a death of the spirit.

ROBERT
(Eagerly.) A death. No; its affirmation! A death! The supreme instant of life from which all coming life
proceeds, the eternal law of nature herself.

RICHARD
And that other law of nature, as you call it: change. How will it be when you turn against her and against me;
when her beauty, or what seems so to you now, wearies you and my affection for you seems false and odious?

ROBERT
That will never be. Never.

RICHARD
And you turn even against yourself for having known me or trafficked with us both?

ROBERT
(Gravely.) It will never be like that, Richard. Be sure of that.

RICHARD
(Contemptuously.) I care very little whether it is or not because there is something I fear much more.

ROBERT
(Shakes his head.) You fear? I disbelieve you, Richard. Since we were boys together I have followed your
mind. You do not know what moral fear is.

RICHARD
(Lays his hand on his arm.) Listen. She is dead. She lies on my bed. I look at her body which I betrayed--
grossly and many times. And loved, too, and wept over. And I know that her body was always my loyal slave.

To me, to me only she gave... *(He breaks off and turns aside, unable to speak.)*
ROBERT
(Softly.) Do not suffer, Richard. There is no need. She is loyal to you, body and soul. Why do you fear?
RICHARD
(Turns towards him, almost fiercely.) Not that fear. But that I will reproach myself then for having taken all
for myself because I would not suffer her to give to another what was hers and not mine to give, because I
accepted from her her loyalty and made her life poorer in love. That is my fear. That I stand between her and
any moments of life that should be hers, between her and you, between her and anyone, between her and
anything. I will not do it. I cannot and I will not. I dare not.
(He leans back in his chair breathless, with shining eyes. Robert rises quietly, and stands behind his chair.)
ROBERT
Look here, Richard. We have said all there is to be said. Let the past be past.
RICHARD
(Quickly and harshly.) Wait. One thing more. For you, too, must know me as I am-- now.
ROBERT
More? Is there more?
RICHARD
I told you that when I saw your eyes this afternoon I felt sad. Your humility and confusion, I felt, united you
to me in brotherhood. *(He turns half round towards him.)* At that moment I felt our whole life together in the
past, and I longed to put my arm around your neck.
ROBERT
(Deeply and suddenly touched.) It is noble of you, Richard, to forgive me like this.
RICHARD
(Struggling with himself.) I told you that I wished you not to do anything false and secret against me-- against

our friendship, against her; not to steal her from me craftily, secretly,
meanly-- in the dark, in the night-- you,
Robert, my friend.

ROBERT
I know. And it was noble of you.
RICHARD
(Looks tip at him with a steady gaze.) No. Not noble. Ignoble.
ROBERT
(Makes an involuntary gesture.) How? Why?
RICHARD
(Looks away again: in a lower voice.) That is what I must tell you
too. Because in the very core of my ignoble
heart I longed to be betrayed by you and by her-- in the dark, in the
night-- secretly, meanly, craftily. By you,
my best friend, and by her. I longed for that passionately and ignobly,
to be dishonoured for ever in love and
in lust, to be...
ROBERT
(Bending down, places his hands over Richard's mouth.) Enough.
Enough. *(He takes his hands away.)* But no.
Go on.
RICHARD
To be for ever a shameful creature and to build up my soul again out
of the ruins of its shame.
ROBERT
And that is why you wished that she...
RICHARD
(With calm.) She has spoken always of her innocence, as I have
spoken always of my guilt, humbling me.
ROBERT
From pride, then?
RICHARD
From pride and from ignoble longing. And from a motive deeper still.
ROBERT
(With decision.) I understand you.

(He returns to his place and begins to speak at once, drawing his chair closer.)
ROBERT

May it not be that we are here and now in the presence of a moment which will free us both-- me as well as
you-- from the last bonds of what is called morality. My friendship for you has laid bonds on me.
RICHARD
Light bonds, apparently.
ROBERT
I acted in the dark, secretly. I will do so no longer. Have you the courage to allow me to act freely?
RICHARD
A duel-- between us?
ROBERT
(With growing excitement.) A battle of both our souls, different as they are, against all that is false in them and
in the world. A battle of your soul against the spectre of fidelity, of mine against the spectre of friendship. All
life is a conquest, the victory of human passion over the commandments of cowardice. Will you, Richard?
Have you the courage? Even if it shatters to atoms the friendship between us, even if it breaks up for ever the
last illusion in your own life? There was an eternity before we were born: another will come after we are dead.
The blinding instant of passion alone-- passion, free, unashamed, irresistible-- that is the only gate by which
we can escape from the misery of what slaves call life. Is not this the language of your own youth that I heard
so often from you in this very place where we are sitting now? Have you changed?
RICHARD
(Passes his hand across his brow.) Yes. It is the language of my youth.
ROBERT

(Eagerly, intensely.) Richard, you have driven me up to this point. She and I have only obeyed your will. You yourself have roused these words in my brain. Your own words. Shall we? Freely? Together?

RICHARD

(Mastering his emotion.) Together no. Fight your part alone. I will not free you. Leave me to fight mine.

ROBERT

(Rises, decided.) You allow me, then?

RICHARD

(Rises also, calmly.) Free yourself.

(A knock is heard at the hall door.)

ROBERT

(In alarm.) What does this mean?

RICHARD

(Calmly.) Bertha, evidently. Did you not ask her to come?

ROBERT

Yes, but... *(Looking about him.)* Then I am going, Richard.

RICHARD

No. I am going.

ROBERT

(Desperately.) Richard, I appeal to you. Let me go. It is over. She is yours. Keep her and forgive me, both of you.

RICHARD

Because you are generous enough to allow me?

ROBERT

(Hotly.) Richard, you will make me angry with you if you say that.

RICHARD

Angry or not, I will not live on your generosity. You have asked her to meet you here tonight and alone. Solve the question between you.

ROBERT

(Promptly.) Open the door. I shall wait in the garden. *(He goes towards the porch.)* Explain to her, Richard, as best you can. I cannot see her now.

RICHARD
I shall go. I tell you. Wait out there if you wish.
*(He goes out by the door on the right. Robert goes out hastily through the porch but comes back the same
instant.)*
ROBERT
An umbrella! *(With a sudden gesture.)* O!
*(He goes out again through the porch. The hall door is heard to open and close. Richard enters, followed by
Bertha, who is dressed in a darkbrown costume, and wears a small dark red hat. She has neither umbrella nor
waterproof.)*
RICHARD

(Gaily.) Welcome back to old Ireland!
BERTHA
(Nervously, seriously.) Is this the place?
RICHARD
Yes, it is. How did you find it?
BERTHA
I told the cabman. I didn't like to ask my way. *(Looking about her curiously.)* Was he not waiting? Has he
gone away?
RICHARD
(Points towards the garden.) He is waiting. Out there. He was waiting when I came.
BERTHA
(Selfpossessed again.) You see, you came after all.
RICHARD
Did you think I would not?
BERTHA
I knew you could not remain away. You see, after all you are like all other men. You had to come. You are
jealous like the others.
RICHARD
You seem annoyed to find me here.
BERTHA

What happened between you?
RICHARD
I told him I knew everything, that I had known for a long time. He
asked how. I said from you.
BERTHA
Does he hate me?
RICHARD
I cannot read in his heart.

BERTHA
(Sits down helplessly.) Yes. He hates me. He believes I made a fool of
him-- betrayed him. I knew he would.
RICHARD
I told him you were sincere with him.
BERTHA
He does not believe it. Nobody would believe it. I should have told
him first-- not you.
RICHARD
I thought he was a common robber, prepared to use even violence
against you. I had to protect you from that.
BERTHA
That I could have done myself.
RICHARD
Are you sure?
BERTHA
It would have been enough to have told him that you knew I was here.
Now I can find out nothing. He hates
me. He is right to hate me. I have treated him badly, shamefully.
RICHARD
(Takes her hand.) Bertha, look at me.
BERTHA
(Turns to him.) Well?
RICHARD
(Gazes into her eyes and then lets her hand fall.) I cannot read in your
heart either.
BERTHA

(Still looking at him.) You could not remain away. Do you not trust me? You can see I am quite calm. I could
have hidden it all from you.
RICHARD
I doubt that.
BERTHA

(With a slight toss of her head.) O, easily if I had wanted to.
RICHARD
(Darkly.) Perhaps you are sorry now that you did not.
BERTHA
Perhaps I am.
RICHARD
(Unpleasantly.) What a fool you were to tell me! It would have been so nice if you had kept it secret.
BERTHA
As you do, no?
RICHARD
As I do, yes. *(He turns to go.)* Goodbye for a while.
BERTHA
(Alarmed, rises.) Are you going?
RICHARD
Naturally. My part is ended here.
BERTHA
To her, I suppose?
RICHARD
(Astonished.) Who?
BERTHA
Her ladyship. I suppose it is all planned so that you may have a good opportunity to meet her and have an
intellectual conversation!
RICHARD
(With an outburst of rude anger.) To meet the devil's father!
BERTHA
(Unpins her hat and sits down.) Very well. You can go. Now I know what to do.
RICHARD

(Returns, approaches her.) You don't believe a word of what you say.
BERTHA
(Calmly.) You can go. Why don't you?
RICHARD
Then you have come here and led him on in this way on account of me. Is that how it is?
BERTHA
There is one person in all this who is not a fool. And that is you. I am though. And he is.
RICHARD
(Continuing.) If so you have indeed treated him badly and shamefully.
BERTHA
(Points at him.) Yes. But it was your fault. And I will end it now. I am simply a tool for you. You have no
respect for me. You never had because I did what I did.
RICHARD
And has he respect?
BERTHA
He has. Of all the persons I met since I came back he is the only one who has. And he knows what they only
suspect. And that is why I liked him from the first and like him still. Great respect for me she has! Why did
you not ask her to come away with you nine years ago?
RICHARD
You know why, Bertha. Ask yourself.
BERTHA
Yes, I know why. You knew the answer you would get. That is why.
RICHARD
That is not why. I did not even ask you.
BERTHA
Yes. You knew I would go, asked or not. I do things. But if I do one thing I can do two things. As I have the
name I can have the gains.
RICHARD

(With increasing excitement.) Bertha, I accept what is to be. I have trusted you. I will trust you still.

BERTHA

To have that against me. To leave me then. *(Almost passionately.)* Why do you not defend me then against
him? Why do you go away from me now without a word? Dick, my God, tell me what you wish me to do?

RICHARD

I cannot, dear. *(Struggling with himself.)* Your own heart will tell you. *(He seizes both her hands.)* I have a
wild delight in my soul, Bertha, as I look at you. I see you as you are yourself. That I came first in your life or
before him then-- that may be nothing to you. You may be his more than mine.

BERTHA

I am not. Only I feel for him, too.

RICHARD

And I do too. You may be his and mine. I will trust you, Bertha, and him too. I must. I cannot hate him since
his arms have been around you. You have drawn us near together. There is something wiser than wisdom in
your heart. Who am I that I should call myself master of your heart or of any woman's? Bertha, love him, be
his, give yourself to him if you desire-- or if you can.

BERTHA

(Dreamily.) I will remain.

RICHARD

Goodbye.

*(He lets her hand fall and goes out rapidly on the right. Bertha remains sitting. Then she rises and goes
timidly towards the porch. She stops near it and, after a little hesitation, calls into the garden.)*

BERTHA

Is anyone out there?

(At the same time she retreats towards the middle of the room. Then she calls again in the same way.)

BERTHA

Is anyone there?
(Robert appears in the open doorway that leads in from the garden. His coat is buttoned and the collar is
turned up. He holds the doorposts with his hands lightly and waits for Bertha to see him.)
BERTHA
(Catching sight of him, starts back: then, quickly.) Robert!

77

ROBERT
Are you alone?
BERTHA
Yes.
ROBERT
(Looking towards the door on the right.) Where is he?
BERTHA
Gone. *(Nervously.)* You startled me. Where did you come from?
ROBERT
(With a movement of his head.) Out there. Did he not tell you I was out there-- waiting?
BERTHA
(Quickly.) Yes, he told me. But I was afraid here alone. With the door open, waiting. *(She comes to the table*
and rests her hand on the corner.) Why do you stand like that in the doorway?
ROBERT
Why? I am afraid too.
BERTHA
Of what?
ROBERT
Of you.
BERTHA
(Looks down.) Do you hate me now?
ROBERT
I fear you. *(Clasping his hands at his back, quietly but a little defiantly.)* I fear a new torture-- a new trap.
BERTHA
(As before.) For what do you blame me?

ROBERT
(Comes forward a few steps, halts: then impulsively:) Why did you
lead me on? Day after day, more and

more. Why did you not stop me? You could have-- with a word. But
not even a word! I forgot myself and
him. You saw it. That I was ruining myself in his eyes, losing his
friendship. Did you want me to?
BERTHA
(Looking up.) You never asked me.
ROBERT
Asked you what?
BERTHA
If he suspected-- or knew.
ROBERT
And would you have told me?
BERTHA
Yes.
ROBERT
(Hesitatingly.) Did you tell him-- everything?
BERTHA
I did.
ROBERT
I mean-- details.
BERTHA
Everything.
ROBERT
(With forced smile.) I see. You were making an experiment for his
sake. On me. Well, why not? It seems I
was a good subject. Still, it was a little cruel of you.
BERTHA
Try to understand me, Robert. You must try.
ROBERT
(With polite gesture.) Well, I will try.

BERTHA

Why do you stand like that near the door? It makes me nervous to look at you.

ROBERT

I am trying to understand. And then I am afraid.

BERTHA

(Holds out her hand.) You need not be afraid.

ROBERT

(Comes towards her quickly and takes her hand. Diffidently:) Used you to laugh over me-- together?

(Drawing his hand away.) But now I must be good or you may laugh over me again-- tonight.

BERTHA

(Distressed, lays her hand on his arm.) Please listen to me, Robert... But you are all wet, drenched! *(She passes her hands over his coat.)* O, you poor fellow! Out there in the rain all that time! I forgot that.

ROBERT

(Laughs.) Yes, you forgot the climate.

BERTHA

But you are really drenched. You must change your coat.

ROBERT

(Takes her hands.) Tell me, it is pity then that you feel for me, as he-- as Richard-- says?

BERTHA

Please change your coat, Robert, when I ask you. You might get a very bad cold from that. Do, please.

ROBERT

What would it matter now?

BERTHA

(Looking round her.) Where do you keep your clothes here?

ROBERT

(Points to the door at the back.) In there. I fancy I have a jacket here. *(Maliciously.)* In my bedroom.

BERTHA

Well, go in and take that off.

ROBERT

And you?
BERTHA
I will wait here for you.
ROBERT
Do you command me to?
BERTHA
(Laughing.) Yes, I command you.
ROBERT
(Promptly.) Then I will. *(He goes quickly towards the bedroom door; then turns round.)* You won't go away?
BERTHA
No, I will wait. But don't be long.
ROBERT
Only a moment.
(He goes into the bedroom, leaving the door open. Bertha looks curiously about her and then glances in indecision towards the door at the back.)
ROBERT
(From the bedroom.) You have not gone?
BERTHA
No.
ROBERT
I am in the dark here. I must light the lamp.
(He is heard striking a match, and putting a glass shade on a lamp. A pink light comes in through the doorway. Bertha glances at her watch at her wristlet and then sits at the table.)
ROBERT
(As before.) Do you like the effect of the light?

BERTHA
O, yes.
ROBERT
Can you admire it from where you are?
BERTHA
Yes, quite well.
ROBERT

It was for you.
BERTHA
(Confused.) I am not worthy even of that.
ROBERT
(Clearly, harshly.) Love's labour lost.
BERTHA
(Rising nervously.) Robert!
ROBERT
Yes?
BERTHA
Come here, quickly! Quickly, I say!
ROBERT
I am ready.
(He appears in the doorway, wearing a dark green velvet jacket.
Seeing her agitation, he comes quickly
towards her.)
ROBERT
What is it, Bertha?
BERTHA
(Trembling.) I was afraid.
ROBERT

Of being alone?
BERTHA
(Catches his hands.) You know what I mean. My nerves are all upset.
ROBERT
That I...?
BERTHA
Promise me, Robert, not to think of such a thing. Never. If you like
me at all. I thought that moment...
ROBERT
What an idea?
BERTHA
But promise me if you like me.
ROBERT
If I like you, Bertha! I promise. Of course, I promise. You are
trembling all over.

BERTHA
Let me sit down somewhere. It will pass in a moment.
ROBERT
My poor Bertha! Sit down. Come.
(He leads her towards a chair near the table. She sits down. He stands beside her.)
ROBERT
(After a short pause.) Has it passed?
BERTHA
Yes. It was only for a moment. I was very silly. I was afraid that... I wanted to see you near me.
ROBERT
That... that you made me promise not to think of?
BERTHA
Yes.

ROBERT
(Keenly.) Or something else?
BERTHA
(Helplessly.) Robert, I feared something. I am not sure what.
ROBERT
And now?
BERTHA
Now you are here. I can see you. Now it has passed.
ROBERT
(With resignation.) Passed. Yes. Love's labour lost.
BERTHA
(Looks up at him.) Listen, Robert. I want to explain to you about that. I could not deceive Dick. Never. In
nothing. I told him everything-- from the first. Then it went on and on; and still you never spoke or asked me.
I wanted you to.
ROBERT
Is that the truth, Bertha?
BERTHA
Yes, because it annoyed me that you could think I was like... like the other women I suppose you knew that

way. I think that Dick is right too. Why should there be secrets?
ROBERT
(Softly.) Still, secrets can be very sweet. Can they not?
BERTHA
(Smiles.) Yes, I know they can. But, you see, I could not keep things
secret from Dick. Besides, what is the
good? They always come out in the end. Is it not better for people to
know?
ROBERT
(Softly and a little shyly.) How could you, Bertha, tell him
everything? Did you? Every single thing that
passed between us?
BERTHA
Yes. Everything he asked me.

ROBERT
Did he ask you-- much?
BERTHA
You know the kind he is. He asks about everything. The ins and outs.
ROBERT
About our kissing, too?
BERTHA
Of course. I told him all.
ROBERT
(Shakes his head slowly.) Extraordinary little person! Were you not
ashamed?
BERTHA
No.
ROBERT
Not a bit?
BERTHA
No. Why? Is that terrible?
ROBERT
And how did he take it? Tell me. I want to know everything, too.
BERTHA
(Laughs.) It excited him. More than usual.
ROBERT

Why? Is he excitable-- still?

BERTHA

(Archly.) Yes, very. When he is not lost in his philosophy.

ROBERT

More than I?

BERTHA

More than you? *(Reflecting.)* How could I answer that? You both are, I suppose?

(Robert turns aside and gazes towards the porch, passing his hand once or twice thoughtfully over his hair.)

BERTHA

(Gently.) Are you angry with me again?

ROBERT

(Moodily.) You are with me.

BERTHA

No, Robert. Why should I?

ROBERT

Because I asked you to come to this place. I tried to prepare it for you. *(He points vaguely here and there.)* A
sense of quietness.

BERTHA

(Touching his jacket with her fingers.) And this, too. Your nice velvet coat.

ROBERT

Also. I will keep no secrets from you.

BERTHA

You remind me of someone in a picture. I like you in it... But you are not angry, are you?

ROBERT

(Darkly.) Yes. That was my mistake. To ask you to come here. I felt it when I looked at you from the garden
and saw you-- you, Bertha-- standing here. *(Hopelessly.)* But what else could I have done?

BERTHA

(Quietly.) You mean because others have been here?

ROBERT

Yes.
(He walks away from her a few paces. A gust of wind makes the lamp on the table flicker. He lowers the wick
slightly.)
BERTHA

(Following him with her eyes.) But I knew that before I came. I am not angry with you for it.
ROBERT
(Shrugs his shoulders.) Why should you be angry with me after all? You are not even angry with him-- for the
same thing-- or worse.
BERTHA
Did he tell you that about himself?
ROBERT
Yes. He told me. We all confess to one another here. Turn about.
BERTHA
I try to forget it.
ROBERT
It does not trouble you?
BERTHA
Not now. Only I dislike to think of it.
ROBERT
It is merely something brutal, you think? Of little importance?
BERTHA
It does not trouble me-- now.
ROBERT
(Looking at her over his shoulder.) But there is something that would trouble you very much and that you
would not try to forget?
BERTHA
What?
ROBERT
(Turning towards her.) If it were not only something brutal with this person or that-- for a few moments. If it
were something fine and spiritual-- with one person only-- with one woman. *(Smiles.)* And perhaps brutal too.

It usually comes to that sooner or later. Would you try to forget and forgive that?
BERTHA

(Toying with her wristlet.) In whom?
ROBERT
In anyone. In me.
BERTHA
(Calmly.) You mean in Dick.
ROBERT
I said in myself. But would you?
BERTHA
You think I would revenge myself? Is Dick not to be free too?
ROBERT
(Points at her.) That is not from your heart, Bertha.
BERTHA
(Proudly.) Yes, it is; let him be free too. He leaves me free also.
ROBERT
(Insistently.) And you know why? And understand? And you like it?
And you want to be? And it makes you
happy? And has made you happy? Always? This gift of freedom
which he gave you-- nine years ago?
BERTHA
(Gazing at him with wide open eyes.) But why do you ask me such a
lot of questions, Robert?
ROBERT
(Stretches out both hands to her.) Because I had another gift to offer
you then-- a common simple gift-- like
myself. If you want to know it I will tell you.
BERTHA
(Looking at her watch.) Past is past, Robert. And I think I ought to go
now. It is nine almost.
ROBERT
(Impetuously.) No, no. Not yet. There is one confession more and we
have the right to speak.
(He crosses before the table rapidly and sits down beside her.)
BERTHA

(Turning towards him, places her left hand on his shoulder.) Yes,
Robert. I know that you like me. You need
not tell me. *(Kindly.)* You need not confess any more tonight.
*(A gust of wind enters through the porch, with a sound of moving
leaves. The lamp flickers quickly.)*
BERTHA
(Pointing over his shoulder.) Look! It is too high.
*(Without rising, he bends towards the table, and turns down the wick
more. The room is half dark. The light
comes in more strongly through the doorway of the bedroom.)*
ROBERT
The wind is rising. I will close that door.
BERTHA
(Listening.) No, it is raining still. It was only a gust of wind.
ROBERT
(Touches her shoulder.) Tell me if the air is too cold for you. *(Half
rising.)* I will close it.
BERTHA
(Detaining him.) No. I am not cold. Besides, I am going now, Robert.
I must.
ROBERT
(Firmly.) No, no. There is no *must* now. We were left here for this.
And you are wrong, Bertha. The past is not
past. It is present here now. My feeling for you is the same now as it
was then, because then-- you slighted it.
BERTHA
No, Robert. I did not.
ROBERT
(Continuing.) You did. And I have felt it all these years without
knowing it-- till now. Even while I lived-- the
kind of life you know and dislike to think of-- the kind of life to
which you condemned me.
BERTHA
I?
ROBERT

Yes, when you slighted the common simple gift I had to offer you--
and took his gift instead.
BERTHA

(Looking at him.) But you never...
ROBERT
No. Because you had chosen him. I saw that. I saw it on the first night
we met, we three together. Why did
you choose him?
BERTHA
(Bends her head.) Is that not love?
ROBERT
(Continuing.) And every night when we two-- he and I-- came to that
corner to meet you I saw it and felt it.
You remember the corner, Bertha?
BERTHA
(As before.) Yes.
ROBERT
And when you and he went away for your walk and I went along the
street alone I felt it. And when he spoke
to me about you and told me he was going away-- then most of all.
BERTHA
Why then most of all?
ROBERT
Because it was then that I was guilty of my first treason towards him.
BERTHA
Robert, what are you saying? Your first treason against Dick?
ROBERT
(Nods.) And not my last. He spoke of you and himself. Of how your
life would be together-- free and all that.
Free, yes! He would not even ask you to go with him. *(Bitterly.)* He
did not. And you went all the same.
BERTHA
I wanted to be with him. You know... *(Raising her head and looking
at him.)* You know how we were then--
Dick and I.
ROBERT

(Unheeding.) I advised him to go alone-- not to take you with him-- to live alone in order to see if what he felt
for you was a passing thing which might ruin your happiness and his career.

BERTHA
Well, Robert. It was unkind of you towards me. But I forgive you because you were thinking of his happiness
and mine.
ROBERT
(Bending closer to her.) No, Bertha. I was not. And that was my treason. I was thinking of myself-- that you
might turn from him when he had gone and he from you. Then I would have offered you my gift. You know
what it was now. The simple common gift that men offer to women. Not the best perhaps. Best or worst-- it
would have been yours.
BERTHA
(Turning away from him.) He did not take your advice.
ROBERT
(As before.) No. And the night you ran away together-- O, how happy I was!
BERTHA
(Pressing his hands.) Keep calm, Robert. I know you liked me always. Why did you not forget me?
ROBERT
(Smiles bitterly.) How happy I felt as I came back along the quays and saw in the distance the boat lit up,
going down the black river, taking you away from me! *(In a calmer tone.)* But why did you choose him? Did
you not like me at all?
BERTHA
Yes. I liked you because you were his friend. We often spoke about you. Often and often. Every time you
wrote or sent papers or books to Dick. And I like you still, Robert. *(Looking into his eyes.)* I never forgot you.
ROBERT

Nor I you. I knew I would see you again. I knew it the night you went away-- that you would come back. And
that was why I wrote and worked to see you again-- here.
BERTHA
And here I am. You were right.
ROBERT
(Slowly.) Nine years. Nine times more beautiful!
BERTHA
(Smiling.) But am I? What do you see in me?

ROBERT
(Gazing at her.) A strange and beautiful lady.
BERTHA
(Almost disgusted.) O, please don't call me such a thing!
ROBERT
(Earnestly.) You are more. A young and beautiful queen.
BERTHA
(With a sudden laugh.) O, Robert!
ROBERT
(Lowering his voice and bending nearer to her.) But do you not know that you are a beautiful human being?
Do you not know that you have a beautiful body? Beautiful and young?
BERTHA
(Gravely.) Some day I will be old.
ROBERT
(Shakes his head.) I cannot imagine it. Tonight you are young and beautiful. Tonight you have come back to
me. *(With passion.)* Who knows what will be tomorrow? I may never see you again or never see you as I do
now.
BERTHA
Would you suffer?
ROBERT
(Looks round the room, without answering.) This room and this hour were made for your coming. When you
have gone-- all is gone.

BERTHA
(Anxiously.) But you will see me again, Robert... as before.
ROBERT
(Looks full at her.) To make him-- Richard-- suffer.
BERTHA
He does not suffer.

ROBERT
(Bowing his head.) Yes, yes. He does.
BERTHA
He knows we like each other. Is there any harm, then?
ROBERT
(Raising his head.) No there is no harm. Why should we not? He does
not know yet what I feel. He has left us
alone here at night, at this hour, because he longs to know it-- he
longs to be delivered.
BERTHA
From what?
ROBERT
(Moves closer to her and presses her arm as he speaks.) From every
law, Bertha, from every bond. All his life
he has sought to deliver himself. Every chain but one he has broken
and that one we are to break. Bertha-- you
and I.
BERTHA
(Almost inaudibly.) Are you sure?
ROBERT
(Still more warmly.) I am sure that no law made by man is sacred
before the impulse of passion. *(Almost
fiercely.)* Who made us for one only? It is a crime against our own
being if we are so. There is no law before
impulse. Laws are for slaves. Bertha, say my name! Let me hear your
voice say it. Softly!
BERTHA
(Softly.) Robert!
ROBERT

(Puts his arm about her shoulder.) Only the impulse towards youth and beauty does not die. *(He points towards the porch.)* Listen!

BERTHA
(In alarm.) What?

ROBERT
The rain falling. Summer rain on the earth. Night rain. The darkness and warmth and flood of passion.
Tonight the earth is loved-- loved and possessed. Her lover's arms around her; and she is silent. Speak, dearest!

BERTHA
(Suddenly leans forward and listens intently.) Hush!

ROBERT
(Listening, smiles.) Nothing. Nobody. We are alone.
(A gust of wind blows in through the porch, with a sound of shaken leaves. The flame of the lamp leaps.)

BERTHA
(Pointing to the lamp.) Look!

ROBERT
Only the wind. We have light enough from the other room.
(He stretches his hand across the table and puts out the lamp. The light from the doorway of the bedroom crosses the place where they sit. The room is quite dark.)

ROBERT
Are you happy? Tell me.

BERTHA
I am going now, Robert. It is very late. Be satisfied.

ROBERT
(Caressing her hair.) Not yet, not yet. Tell me, do you love me a little?

BERTHA
I like you, Robert. I think you are good. *(Half rising.)* Are you satisfied?

ROBERT

(Detaining her, kisses her hair.) Do not go, Bertha! There is time still.
Do you love me too? I have waited a
long time. Do you love us both-- him and also me? Do you, Bertha?
The truth! Tell me. Tell me with your
eyes. Or speak!
(She does not answer. In the silence the rain is heard falling.)
Third Act
*(The drawingroom of Richard Rowan's house at Merrion. The folding
doors at the right are closed and also
the double doors leading to the garden. The green plush curtains are
drawn across the window on the left.
The room is half dark. It is early in the morning of the next day.
Bertha sits beside the window looking out
between the curtains. She wears a loose saffron dressing gown. Her
hair is combed loosely over the ears and
knotted at the neck. Her hands are folded in her lap. Her face is pale
and drawn.)*

*(Brigid comes in through the folding doors on the right with a
featherbroom and duster. She is about to cross
but, seeing Bertha, she halts suddenly and blesses herself
instinctively.)*
BRIGID
Merciful hour, ma'am. You put the heart across me. Why did you get
up so early?
BERTHA
What time is it?
BRIGID
After seven, ma'am. Are you long up?
BERTHA
Some time.
BRIGID
(Approaching her.) Had you a bad dream that woke you?
BERTHA
I didn't sleep all night. So I got up to see the sun rise.
BRIGID

(Opens the double doors.) It's a lovely morning now after all the rain we had. *(Turns round.)* But you must be
dead tired, ma'am. What will the master say at your doing a thing like that? *(She goes to the door of the study*
and knocks.) Master Richard!
BERTHA
(Looks round.) He is not there. He went out an hour ago.
BRIGID
Out there, on the strand, is it?
BERTHA
Yes.
BRIGID
(Comes towards her and leans over the back of a chair.) Are you fretting yourself, ma'am, about anything?
BERTHA
No, Brigid.

BRIGID
Don't be. He was always like that, meandering off by himself somewhere. He is a curious bird, Master
Richard, and always was. Sure there isn't a turn in him I don't know. Are you fretting now maybe because he
does be in there *(pointing to the study)* half the night at his books? Leave him alone. He'll come back to you
again. Sure he thinks the sun shines out of your face, ma'am.
BERTHA
(Sadly.) That time is gone.
BRIGID
(Confidentially.) And good cause I have to remember it-- that time when he was paying his addresses to you.
(She sits down beside Bertha. In a lower voice.) Do you know that he used to tell me all about you and
nothing to his mother, God rest her soul? Your letters and all.
BERTHA
What? My letters to him?
BRIGID

(Delighted.) Yes. I can see him sitting on the kitchen table, swinging his legs and spinning out of him yards of
talk about you and him and Ireland and all kinds of devilment-- to an ignorant old woman like me. But that
was always his way. But if he had to meet a grand highup person he'd be twice as grand himself. *(Suddenly
looks at Bertha.)* Is it crying you are now? Ah, sure, don't cry. There's good times coming still.
BERTHA
No, Brigid, that time comes only once in a lifetime. The rest of life is good for nothing except to remember
that time.
BRIGID
(Is silent for a moment: then says kindly:) Would you like a cup of tea, ma'am? That would make you all right.
BERTHA
Yes, I would. But the milkman has not come yet.
BRIGID
No. Master Archie told me to wake him before he came. He's going out for a jaunt in the car. But I've a cup
left overnight. I'll have the kettle boiling in a jiffy. Would you like a nice egg with it?
BERTHA
No, thanks.
BRIGID

Or a nice bit of toast?
BERTHA
No, Brigid, thanks. Just a cup of tea.
BRIGID
(Crossing to the folding doors.) I won't be a moment. *(She stops, turns back and goes towards the door on the
left.)* But first I must waken Master Archie or there'll be ructions. *(She goes out by the door on the left. After a few moments Bertha rises and goes over to the study. She opens
the door wide and looks in. One can see a small untidy room with many bookshelves and a large writingtable*

with papers and an extinguished lamp and before it a padded chair. She remains standing for some time in the doorway, then closes the door again without entering the room. She returns to her chair by the window and sits down. Archie, dressed as before, comes in by the door on the right, followed by Brigid.)

ARCHIE

(Comes to her and, putting up his face to be kissed, says:) Buon giorno, mamma!

BERTHA

(Kissing him.) Buon giorno, Archie! *(To Brigid.)* Did you put another vest on him under that one?

BRIGID

He wouldn't let me, ma'am.

ARCHIE

I'm not cold, mamma.

BERTHA

I said you were to put it on, didn't I?

ARCHIE

But where is the cold?

BERTHA

(Takes a comb from her head and combs his hair back at both sides.) And the sleep is in your eyes still.

BRIGID

He went to bed immediately after you went out last night, ma'am.

ARCHIE

You know he's going to let me drive, mamma.

BERTHA

(Replacing the comb in her hair, embraces him suddenly.) O, what a big man to drive a horse!

BRIGID

Well, he's daft on horses, anyhow.

ARCHIE

(Releasing himself.) I'll make him go quick. You will see from the window, mamma. With the whip. *(He

makes the gesture of cracking a whip and shouts at the top of his voice.) Avanti!
BRIGID
Beat the poor horse, is it?
BERTHA
Come here till I clean your mouth. *(She takes her handkerchief from the pocket of her gown, wets it with her*
tongue and cleans his mouth.) You're all smudges or something, dirty little creature you are.
ARCHIE
(Repeats, laughing.) Smudges! What is smudges?
(The noise is heard of a milkcan rattled on the railings before the window.)
BRIGID
(Draws aside the curtains and looks out.) Here he is!
ARCHIE
(Rapidly.) Wait. I'm ready. Goodbye, mamma! *(He kisses her hastily and turns to go.)* Is pappie up?
BRIGID
(Takes him by the arm.) Come on with you now.
BERTHA
Mind yourself, Archie, and don't be long or I won't let you go any more.
ARCHIE
All right. Look out of the window and you'll see me. Goodbye.
(Brigid and Archie go out by the door on the left. Bertha stands up and, drawing aside the curtains still more,
stands in the embrasure of the window looking out. The hall door is heard opening: then a slight noise of
voices and cans is heard. The door is closed. After a moment or two Bertha is seen waving her hand gaily in a
salute. Brigid enters and stands behind her, looking over her shoulder.)

BRIGID
Look at the sit of him! As serious as you like.
BERTHA

(Suddenly withdrawing from her post.) Stand out of the window. I
don't want to be seen.
BRIGID
Why, ma'am, what is it?
BERTHA
(Crossing towards the folding doors.) Say I'm not up, that I'm not
well. I can't see anyone.
BRIGID
(Follows her.) Who is it, ma'am?
BERTHA
(Halting.) Wait a moment.
(She listens. A knock is heard at the hall door.)
BERTHA
(Stands a moment in doubt, then.) No, say I'm in.
BRIGID
(In doubt.) Here?
BERTHA
(Hurriedly.) Yes. Say I have just got up.
*(Brigid goes out on the left. Bertha goes towards the double doors
and fingers the curtains nervously, as if
settling them. The hall door is heard to open. Then Beatrice Justice
enters and, as Bertha does not turn at
once, stands in hesitation near the door on the left. She is dressed as
before and has a newspaper in her
hand.)*
BEATRICE
(Advances rapidly.) Mrs Rowan, excuse me for coming at such an
hour.
BERTHA
(Turns.) Good morning, Miss Justice. *(She comes towards her.)* Is
anything the matter?
BEATRICE

(Nervously.) I don't know. That is what I wanted to ask you.
BERTHA
(Looks curiously at her.) You are out of breath. Won't you sit down?
BEATRICE

(Sitting down.) Thank you.

BERTHA

(Sits opposite her, pointing to her paper.) Is there something in the paper?

BEATRICE

(Laughs nervously: opens the paper.) Yes.

BERTHA

About Dick?

BEATRICE

Yes. Here it is. A long article, a leading article, by my cousin. All his life is here. Do you wish to see it?

BERTHA

(Takes the paper, and opens it.) Where is it?

BEATRICE

In the middle. It is headed: *A Distinguished Irishman.*

BERTHA

Is it... for Dick or against him?

BEATRICE

(Warmly.) O, for him! You can read what he says about Mr Rowan. And I know that Robert stayed in town
very late last night to write it.

BERTHA

(Nervously.) Yes. Are you sure?

BEATRICE

Yes. Very late. I heard him come home. It was long after two.

BERTHA

(Watching her.) It alarmed you? I mean to be awakened at that hour of the morning.

BEATRICE

I am a light sleeper. But I knew he had come from the office and then... I suspected he had written an article
about Mr Rowan and that was why he came so late.

BERTHA

How quick you were to think of that!

BEATRICE

Well, after what took place here yesterday afternoon-- I mean what
Robert said, that Mr Rowan had accepted
this position. It was only natural I should think...
BERTHA
Ah, yes. Naturally.
BEATRICE
(Hastily.) But that is not what alarmed me. But immediately after I
heard a noise in my cousin's room.
BERTHA
(Crumples together the paper in her hands, breathlessly.) My God!
What is it? Tell me.
BEATRICE
(Observing her.) Why does that upset you so much?
BERTHA
(Sinking back, with a forced laugh.) Yes, of course, it is very foolish
of me. My nerves are all upset. I slept
very badly, too. That is why I got up so early. But tell me what was it
then?
BEATRICE
Only the noise of his valise being pulled along the floor. Then I heard
him walking about his room, whistling
softly. And then locking it and strapping it.
BERTHA
He is going away!
BEATRICE
That was what alarmed me. I feared he had had a quarrel with Mr
Rowan and that his article was an attack.
BERTHA

But why should they quarrel? Have you noticed anything between
them?
BEATRICE
I thought I did. A coldness.
BERTHA
Lately?
BEATRICE
For some time past.

BERTHA
(Smoothing the paper out.) Do you know the reason?
BEATRICE
(Hesitatingly.) No.
BERTHA
(After a pause.) Well, but if this article is for him, as you say, they have not quarrelled. (She reflects a
moment.) And written last night, too.
BEATRICE
Yes. I bought the paper at once to see. But why, then, is he going away so suddenly? I feel that there is
something wrong. I feel that something has happened between them.
BERTHA
Would you be sorry?
BEATRICE
I would be very sorry. You see, Mrs Rowan, Robert is my first cousin and it would grieve me very deeply if
he were to treat Mr Rowan badly, now that he has come back, or if they had a serious quarrel especially
because...
BERTHA
(Toying with the paper.) Because?
BEATRICE
Because it was my cousin who urged Mr Rowan always to come back. I have that on my conscience.
BERTHA

It should be on Mr Hand's conscience, should it not?
BEATRICE
(Uncertainly.) On mine, too. Because-- I spoke to my cousin about Mr Rowan when he was away and, to a
certain extent, it was I...
BERTHA
(Nods slowly.) I see. And that is on your conscience. Only that?
BEATRICE
I think so.
BERTHA

(Almost cheerfully.) It looks as if it was you, Miss Justice, who brought my husband back to Ireland.

BEATRICE

I, Mrs Rowan?

BERTHA

Yes, you. By your letters to him and then by speaking to your cousin as you said just now. Do you not think
that you are the person who brought him back?

BEATRICE

(Blushing suddenly.) No. I could not think that.

BERTHA

(Watches her for a moment; then turning aside.) You know that my husband is writing very much since he
came back.

BEATRICE

Is he?

BERTHA

Did you not know? *(She points towards the study.)* He passes the greater part of the night in there writing.
Night after night.

BEATRICE

In his study?

BERTHA

Study or bedroom. You may call it what you please. He sleeps there, too, on a sofa. He slept there last night. I
can show you if you don't believe me.

(She rises to go towards the study. Beatrice half rises quickly and makes a gesture of refusal.)

BEATRICE

I believe you, of course, Mrs Rowan, when you tell me.

BERTHA

(Sitting down again.) Yes. He is writing. And it must be about something which has come into his life lately--
since we came back to Ireland. Some change. Do you know that any change has come into his life? *(She looks
searchingly at her.)* Do you know it or feel it?

BEATRICE
(Answers her look steadily.) Mrs Rowan, that is not a question to ask
me. If any change has come into his life
since he came back you must know and feel it.
BERTHA
You could know it just as well. You are very intimate in this house.
BEATRICE
I am not the only person who is intimate here.
(They both look at each other coldly in silence for some moments.
Bertha lays aside the paper and sits down
on a chair nearer to Beatrice.)
BERTHA
(Placing her hand on Beatrice's knee.) So you also hate me, Miss
Justice?
BEATRICE
(With an effort.) Hate you? I?
BERTHA
(Insistently but softly.) Yes. You know what it means to hate a
person?
BEATRICE
Why should I hate you? I have never hated anyone.
BERTHA
Have you ever loved anyone? (She puts her hand on Beatrice's wrist.)
Tell me. You have?
BEATRICE

(Also softly.) Yes. In the past.
BERTHA
Not now?
BEATRICE
No.
BERTHA
Can you say that to me-- truly? Look at me.
BEATRICE
(Looks at her.) Yes, I can.
(A short pause. Bertha withdraws her hand, and turns away her head
in some embarrassment.)

BERTHA
You said just now that another person is intimate in this house. You meant your cousin... Was it he?
BEATRICE
Yes.
BERTHA
Have you not forgotten him?
BEATRICE
(Quietly.) I have tried to.
BERTHA
(Clasping her hands.) You hate me. You think I am happy. If you only knew how wrong you are!
BEATRICE
(Shakes her head.) I do not.
BERTHA
Happy! When I do not understand anything that he writes, when I cannot help him in any way, when I don't
even understand half of what he says to me sometimes! You could and you can. (Excitedly.) But I am afraid
for him, afraid for both of them. (She stands up suddenly and goes towards the davenport.) He must not go
away like that. (She takes a writing pad from the drawer and writes a few lines in great haste.) No, it is
impossible! Is he mad to do such a thing? (Turning to Beatrice.) Is he still at home?

BEATRICE
(Watching her in wonder.) Yes. Have you written to him to ask him to come here?
BERTHA
(Rises.) I have. I will send Brigid across with it. Brigid! (She goes out by the door on the left rapidly.)
BEATRICE
(Gazing after her, instinctively:) It is true, then!
(She glances toward the door of Richard's study and catches her head in her hands. Then, recovering herself,

she takes the paper from the little table, opens it, takes a spectacle case from her handbag and, putting on a
pair of spectacles, bends down, reading it. Richard Rowan enters from the garden. He is dressed as before but
wears a soft hat and carries a thin cane.)

RICHARD

(Stands in the doorway, observing her for some moments.) There are demons *(he points out towards the*
strand) out there. I heard them jabbering since dawn.

BEATRICE

(Starts to her feet.) Mr Rowan!

RICHARD

I assure you. The isle is full of voices. Yours also. *Otherwise I could not see you,* it said. And her voice. But, I
assure you, they are all demons. I made the sign of the cross upside down and that silenced them.

BEATRICE

(Stammering.) I came here, Mr Rowan, so early because... to show you this... Robert wrote it... about you...
last night.

RICHARD

(Takes off his hat.) My dear Miss Justice, you told me yesterday, I think, why you came here and I never
forget anything. *(Advancing towards her, holding out his hand.)* Good morning.

BEATRICE

(Suddenly takes of her spectacles and places the paper in his hands.) I came for this. It is an article about you.
Robert wrote it last night. Will you read it?

RICHARD

(Bows.) Read it now? Certainly.

BEATRICE

(Looks at him in despair.) O, Mr Rowan, it makes me suffer to look at you.

RICHARD

(Opens and reads the paper.) Death of the Very Reverend Canon Mulhall. Is that it?

(Bertha appears at the door on the left and stands to listen.)

RICHARD

(Turns over a page.) Yes, here we are! *A Distinguished Irishman. (He begins to read in a rather loud hard voice.)* Not the least vital of the problems which confront our country is the problem of her attitude towards those of her children who, having left her in her hour of need, have been called back to her now on the eve of her longawaited victory, to her whom in loneliness and exile they have at last learned to love. In exile, we have said, but here we must distinguish. There is an economic and there is a spiritual exile. There are those who left her to seek the bread by which men live and there are others, nay, her most favoured children, who left her to seek in other lands that food of the spirit by which a nation of human beings is sustained in life. Those who recall the intellectual life of Dublin of a decade since will have many memories of Mr Rowan. Something of that fierce indignation which lacerated the heart...

(He raises his eyes from the paper and sees Bertha standing in the doorway. Then he lays aside the paper and looks at her. A long silence.)

BEATRICE

(With an effort.) You see, Mr Rowan, your day has dawned at last. Even here. And you see that you have a warm friend in Robert, a friend who understands you.

RICHARD

Did you notice the little phrase at the beginning: *those who left her in her hour of need?*

(He looks searchingly at Bertha, turns and walks into his study, closing the door behind him.)

BERTHA

(Speaking half to herself.) I gave up everything for him, religion, family, my own peace.

(She sits down heavily in an armchair. Beatrice comes towards her.)

BEATRICE
(Weakly.) But do you not feel also that Mr Rowan's ideas...
BERTHA
(Bitterly.) Ideas and ideas! But the people in this world have other ideas or pretend to. They have to put up
with him in spite of his ideas because he is able to do something. Me, no. I am nothing.
BEATRICE
You stand by his side.

BERTHA
(With increasing bitterness.) Ah, nonsense, Miss Justice! I am only a thing he got entangled with and my son
is-- the nice name they give those children. Do you think I am a stone? Do you think I don't see it in their eyes
and in their manner when they have to meet me?
BEATRICE
Do not let them humble you, Mrs Rowan.
BERTHA
(Haughtily.) Humble me! I am very proud of myself, if you want to know. What have they ever done for him?
I made him a man. What are they all in his life? No more than the dirt under his boots! (She stands up and
walks excitedly to and fro.) He can despise me, too, like the rest of them-- now. And you can despise me. But
you will never humble me, any of you.
BEATRICE
Why do you accuse me?
BERTHA
(Going to her impulsively.) I am in such suffering. Excuse me if I was rude. I want us to be friends. (She holds
out her hands.) Will you?
BEATRICE
(Taking her hands.) Gladly.
BERTHA
(Looking at her.) What lovely long eyelashes you have! And your eyes have such a sad expression!

BEATRICE
(Smiling.) I see very little with them. They are very weak.
BERTHA
(Warmly.) But beautiful.
(She embraces her quietly and kisses her. Then withdraws from her a little shyly. Brigid comes in from the left.)
BRIGID
I gave it to himself, ma'am.
BERTHA
Did he send a message?

BRIGID
He was just going out, ma'am. He told me to say he'd be here after me.
BERTHA
Thanks.
BRIGID
(Going.) Would you like the tea and the toast now, ma'am?
BERTHA
Not now, Brigid. After perhaps. When Mr Hand comes show him in at once.
BRIGID
Yes, ma'am. *(She goes out on the left.)*
BEATRICE
I will go now, Mrs Rowan, before he comes.
BERTHA
(Somewhat timidly.) Then we are friends?
BEATRICE
(In the same tone.) We will try to be. *(Turning.)* Do you allow me to go out through the garden? I don't want
to meet my cousin now.
BERTHA
Of course. *(She takes her hand.)* It is so strange that we spoke like this now. But I always wanted to. Did you?
BEATRICE
I think I did, too.

BERTHA
(Smiling.) Even in Rome. When I went out for a walk with Archie I used to think about you, what you were
like, because I knew about you from Dick. I used to look at different persons, coming out of churches or going
by in carriages, and think that perhaps they were like you. Because Dick told me you were dark.
BEATRICE
(Again nervously.) Really?
BERTHA

(Pressing her hand.) Goodbye then-- for the present.
BEATRICE
(Disengaging her hand.) Good morning.
BERTHA
I will see you to the gate.
(She accompanies her out through the double doors. They go down through the garden. Richard Rowan
comes in from the study. He halts near the doors, looking down the garden. Then he turns away, comes to the
little table, takes up the paper and reads. Bertha, after some moments, appears in the doorway and stands
watching him till he has finished. He lays down the paper again and turns to go back to his study.)
BERTHA
Dick!
RICHARD
(Stopping.) Well?
BERTHA
You have not spoken to me.
RICHARD
I have nothing to say. Have you?
BERTHA
Do you not wish to know-- about what happened last night?
RICHARD
That I will never know.
BERTHA

I will tell you if you ask me.

RICHARD

You will tell me. But I will never know. Never in this world.

BERTHA

(Moving towards him.) I will tell you the truth, Dick, as I always told you. I never lied to you.

RICHARD

(Clenching his hands in the air, passionately.) Yes, yes. The truth! But I will never know, I tell you.

BERTHA

Why, then, did you leave me last night?

RICHARD

(Bitterly.) In your hour of need.

BERTHA

(Threateningly.) You urged me to it. Not because you love me. If you loved me or if you knew what love was
you would not have left me. For your own sake you urged me to it.

RICHARD

I did not make myself. I am what I am.

BERTHA

To have it always to throw against me. To make me humble before you, as you always did. To be free
yourself. *(Pointing towards the garden.)* With her! And that is your love! Every word you say is false.

RICHARD

(Controlling himself.) It is useless to ask you to listen to me.

BERTHA

Listen to you! She is the person for listening. Why would you waste your time with me? Talk to her.

RICHARD

(Nods his head.) I see. You have driven her away from me now, as you drove everyone else from my side--
every friend I ever had, every human being that ever tried to approach me. You hate her.

BERTHA

(Warmly.) No such thing! I think you have made her unhappy as you have made me and as you made your
dead mother unhappy and killed her. Woman-killer! That is your name.

RICHARD

(Turns to go.) Arrivederci!

BERTHA

(Excitedly.) She is a fine and high character. I like her. She is everything that I am not-- in birth and education.
You tried to ruin her but you could not. Because she is well able for you-- what I am not. And you know it.

RICHARD

(Almost shouting.) What the devil are you talking about her for?

BERTHA

(Clasping her hands.) O, how I wish I had never met you! How I curse that day!

RICHARD

(Bitterly.) I am in the way, is it? You would like to be free now. You have only to say the word.

BERTHA

(Proudly.) Whenever you like I am ready.

RICHARD

So that you could meet your lover-- freely?

BERTHA

Yes.

RICHARD

Night after night?

BERTHA

(Gazing before her and speaking with intense passion.) To meet my lover! *(Holding out her arms before her.)*
My lover! Yes! My lover!
(She bursts suddenly into tears and sinks down on a chair, covering her face with her hands. Richard
approaches her slowly and touches her on the shoulder.)

RICHARD

Bertha! *(She does not answer.)* Bertha, you are free.

BERTHA

(Pushes his hand aside and starts to her feet.) Don't touch me! You are a stranger to me. You do not
understand anything in me-- not one thing in my heart or soul. A stranger! I am living with a stranger!
(A knock is heard at the hall door. Bertha dries her eyes quickly with her handkerchief and settles the front of
her gown. Richard listens for a moment, looks at her keenly and, turning away, walks into his study. Robert
Hand enters from the left. He is dressed in dark brown and carries in his hand a brown Alpine hat.)
ROBERT

(Closing the door quietly behind him.) You sent for me.
BERTHA

(Rises.) Yes. Are you mad to think of going away like that-- without even coming here-- without saying
anything?
ROBERT

(Advancing towards the table on which the paper lies, glances at it.) What I have to say I said here.
BERTHA

When did you write it? Last night-- after I went away?
ROBERT

(Gracefully.) To be quite accurate, I wrote part of it-- in my mind-- before you went away. The rest-- the
worst part-- I wrote after. Much later.
BERTHA

And you could write last night!
ROBERT

(Shrugs his shoulders.) I am a welltrained animal. *(He comes closer to her.)* I passed a long wandering night
after... in my office, at the vicechancellor's house, in a nightclub, in the streets, in my room. Your image was
always before my eyes, your hand in my hand. Bertha, I will never forget last night. *(He lays his hat on the*

table and takes her hand.) Why do you not look at me? May I not touch you?

BERTHA

(Points to the study.) Dick is in there.

ROBERT

(Drops her hand.) In that case children be good.

BERTHA

Where are you going?

ROBERT

To foreign parts. That is, to my cousin Jack Justice, *alias* Doggy Justice, in Surrey. He has a nice country
place there and the air is mild.

BERTHA

Why are you going?

ROBERT

(Looks at her in silence.) Can you not guess one reason?

BERTHA

On account of me?

ROBERT

Yes. It is not pleasant for me to remain here just now.

BERTHA

(Sits down helplessly.) But this is cruel of you, Robert. Cruel to me and to him also.

ROBERT

Has he asked... what happened?

BERTHA

(Joining her hands in despair.) No. He refuses to ask me anything. He says he will never know.

ROBERT

(Nods gravely.) Richard is right there. He is always right.

BERTHA

But, Robert, you must speak to him.

ROBERT

What am I to say to him?

BERTHA

The truth! Everything!

ROBERT
(Reflects.) No, Bertha. I am a man speaking to a man. I cannot tell
him everything.
BERTHA
He will believe that you are going away because you are afraid to face
him after last night.
ROBERT
(After a pause.) Well, I am not a coward any more than he. I will see
him.
BERTHA
(Rises.) I will call him.

ROBERT
(Catching her hands.) Bertha! What happened last night? What is the
truth that I am to tell? *(He gazes
earnestly into her eyes.)* Were you mine in that sacred night of love?
Or have I dreamed it?
BERTHA
(Smiles faintly.) Remember your dream of me. You dreamed that I
was yours last night.
ROBERT
And that is the truth-- a dream? That is what I am to tell?
BERTHA
Yes.
ROBERT
(Kisses both her hands.) Bertha! *(In a softer voice.)* In all my life only
that dream is real. I forget the rest. *(He
kisses her hands again.)* And now I can tell him the truth. Call him.
*(Bertha goes to the door of Richard's study and knocks. There is no
answer. She knocks again.)*
BERTHA
Dick! *(There is no answer.)* Mr Hand is here. He wants to speak to
you, to say goodbye. He is going away.
*(There is no answer. She beats her hand loudly on the panel of the
door and calls in an alarmed voice.)* Dick!
Answer me!

(Richard Rowan comes in from the study. He comes at once to Robert but does not hold out his hand.)

RICHARD

(Calmly.) I thank you for your kind article about me. Is it true that you have come to say goodbye?

ROBERT

There is nothing to thank me for, Richard. Now and always I am your friend. Now more than ever before. Do
you believe me, Richard?

*(Richard sits down on a chair and buries his face in his hands. Bertha and Robert gaze at each other in
silence. Then she turns away and goes out quietly on the right. Robert goes towards Richard and stands near
him, resting his hands on the back of a chair, looking down at him. There is a long silence. A fishwoman is
heard crying out as she passes along the road outside.)*

THE FISHWOMAN

Fresh Dublin bay herrings! Fresh Dublin bay herrings! Dublin bay herrings!

ROBERT

(Quietly.) I will tell you the truth, Richard. Are you listening?

RICHARD

(Raises his face and leans back to listen.) Yes.

(Robert sits on the chair beside him. The fishwoman is heard calling out farther away.)

THE FISHWOMAN

Fresh herrings! Dublin bay herrings!

ROBERT

I failed, Richard. That is the truth. Do you believe me?

RICHARD

I am listening.

ROBERT

I failed. She is yours, as she was nine years ago, when you met her first.

RICHARD

When we met her first, you mean.

ROBERT
Yes. *(He looks down for some moments.)* Shall I go on?
RICHARD
Yes.
ROBERT
She went away. I was left alone-- for the second time. I went to the vicechancellor's house and dined. I said
you were ill and would come another night. I made epigrams new and old-- that one about the statues also. I
drank claret cup. I went to my office and wrote my article. Then...
RICHARD
Then?
ROBERT
Then I went to a certain nightclub. There were men there-- and also women. At least, they looked like women.
I danced with one of them. She asked me to see her home. Shall I go on?
RICHARD

Yes.
ROBERT
I saw her home in a cab. She lives near Donnybrook. In the cab took place what the subtle Duns Scotus calls a
death of the spirit. Shall I go on?
RICHARD
Yes.
ROBERT
She wept. She told me she was the divorced wife of a barrister. I offered her a sovereign as she told me she
was short of money. She would not take it and wept very much. Then she drank some melissa water from a
little bottle which she had in her satchel. I saw her enter her house. Then I walked home. In my room I found
that my coat was all stained with the melissa water. I had no luck even with my coats yesterday: that was the
second one. The idea came to me then to change my suit and go away by the morning boat. I packed my valise

and went to bed. I am going away by the next train to my cousin, Jack
Justice, in Surrey. Perhaps for a
fortnight. Perhaps longer. Are you disgusted?
RICHARD
Why did you not go by the boat?
ROBERT
I slept it out.
RICHARD
You intended to go without saying goodbye-- without coming here?
ROBERT
Yes.
RICHARD
Why?
ROBERT
My story is not very nice, is it?
RICHARD
But you have come.
ROBERT
Bertha sent me a message to come.

RICHARD
But for that...?
ROBERT
But for that I should not have come.
RICHARD
Did it strike you that if you had gone without coming here I should
have understood it-- in my own way?
ROBERT
Yes, it did.
RICHARD
What, then, do you wish me to believe?
ROBERT
I wish you to believe that I failed. That Bertha is yours now as she
was nine years ago, when you-- when we--
met her first.
RICHARD
Do you want to know what I did?

ROBERT
No.
RICHARD
I came home at once.
ROBERT
Did you hear Bertha return?
RICHARD
No. I wrote all the night. And thought. *(Pointing to the study.)* In
there. Before dawn I went out and walked
the strand from end to end.
ROBERT
(Shaking his head.) Suffering. Torturing yourself.
RICHARD

Hearing voices about me. The voices of those who say they love me.
ROBERT
(Points to the door on the right.) One. And mine?
RICHARD
Another still.
ROBERT
(Smiles and touches his forehead with his right forefinger.) True. My
interesting but somewhat melancholy
cousin. And what did they tell you?
RICHARD
They told me to despair.
ROBERT
A queer way of showing their love, I must say! And will you despair?
RICHARD
(Rising.) No.
*(A noise is heard at the window. Archie's face is seen flattened
against one of the panes. He is heard calling.)*
ARCHIE
Open the window! Open the window!
ROBERT
(Looks at Richard.) Did you hear his voice, too, Richard, with the
others-- out there on the strand? Your son's
voice. *(Smiling.)* Listen! How full it is of despair!

ARCHIE
Open the window, please, will you?
ROBERT
Perhaps, there, Richard, is the freedom we seek-- you in one way, I in another. In him and not in us. Perhaps...
RICHARD
Perhaps...?
ROBERT
I said *perhaps*. I would say almost surely if...
RICHARD
If what?
ROBERT
(With a faint smile.) If he were mine.
(He goes to the window and opens it. Archie scrambles in.)
ROBERT
Like yesterday-- eh?
ARCHIE
Good morning, Mr Hand. *(He runs to Richard and kisses him:)* Buon giorno, babbo.
RICHARD
Buon giorno, Archie.
ROBERT
And where were you, my young gentleman?
ARCHIE
Out with the milkman. I drove the horse. We went to Booterstown. *(He takes off his cap and throws it on a chair.)* I am very hungry.
ROBERT
(Takes his hat from the table.) Richard, goodbye. *(Offering his hand.)* To our next meeting!
RICHARD
(Rises, touches his hand.) Goodbye.
(Bertha appears at the door on the right.)
ROBERT
(Catches sight of her: to Archie.) Get your cap. Come on with me. I'll buy you a cake and I'll tell you a story.
ARCHIE

(To Bertha.) May I, mamma?

BERTHA

Yes.

ARCHIE

(Takes his cap.) I am ready.

ROBERT

(To Richard and Bertha.) Goodbye to pappa and mamma. But not a big goodbye.

ARCHIE

Will you tell me a fairy story, Mr Hand?

ROBERT

A fairy story? Why not? I am your fairy godfather.

(They go out together through the double doors and down the garden. When they have gone Bertha goes to
Richard and puts her arm round his waist.)

BERTHA

Dick, dear, do you believe now that I have been true to you? Last night and always?

RICHARD

(Sadly.) Do not ask me, Bertha.

BERTHA

(Pressing him more closely.) I have been, dear. Surely you believe me. I gave you myself-- all. I gave up all
for you. You took me-- and you left me.

RICHARD

When did I leave you?

BERTHA

You left me: and I waited for you to come back to me. Dick, dear, come here to me. Sit down. How tired you
must be!

(She draws him towards the lounge. He sits down, almost reclining, resting on his arm. She sits on the mat
before the lounge, holding his hand.)

BERTHA

Yes, dear. I waited for you. Heavens, what I suffered then-- when we lived in Rome! Do you remember the

terrace of our house?
RICHARD

Yes.
BERTHA
I used to sit there, waiting, with the poor child with his toys, waiting till he got sleepy. I could see all the roofs
of the city and the river, the *Tevere.* What is its name?
RICHARD
The Tiber.
BERTHA
(Caressing her cheek with his hand.) It was lovely, Dick, only I was so sad. I was alone, Dick, forgotten by
you and by all. I felt my life was ended.
RICHARD
It had not begun.
BERTHA
And I used to look at the sky, so beautiful, without a cloud and the city you said was so old: and then I used to
think of Ireland and about ourselves.
RICHARD
Ourselves?
BERTHA
Yes. Ourselves. Not a day passes that I do not see ourselves, you and me, as we were when we met first.
Every day of my life I see that. Was I not true to you all that time?
RICHARD
(Sighs deeply.) Yes, Bertha. You were my bride in exile.
BERTHA
Wherever you go, I will follow you. If you wish to go away now I will go with you.
RICHARD
I will remain. It is too soon yet to despair.
BERTHA
(Again caressing his hand.) It is not true that I want to drive everyone from you. I wanted to bring you close

together-- you and him. Speak to me. Speak out all your heart to me. What you feel and what you suffer.
RICHARD

I am wounded, Bertha.
BERTHA
How wounded, dear? Explain to me what you mean. I will try to understand everything you say. In what way
are you wounded?
RICHARD
(Releases his hand and, taking her head between his hands, bends it back and gazes long into her eyes.) I
have a deep, deep wound of doubt in my soul.
BERTHA
(Motionless.) Doubt of me?
RICHARD
Yes.
BERTHA
I am yours. *(In a whisper.)* If I died this moment, I am yours.
RICHARD
(Still gazing at her and speaking as if to an absent person.) I have wounded my soul for you-- a deep wound
of doubt which can never be healed. I can never know, never in this world. I do not wish to know or to
believe. I do not care. It is not in the darkness of belief that I desire you. But in restless living wounding
doubt. To hold you by no bonds, even of love, to be united with you in body and soul in utter nakedness-- for
this I longed. And now I am tired for a while, Bertha. My wound tires me.
(He stretches himself out wearily along the lounge. Bertha holds his hand, still speaking very softly.)
BERTHA
Forget me, Dick. Forget me and love me again as you did the first time. I want my lover. To meet him, to go
to him, to give myself to him. You, Dick. O, my strange wild lover, come back to me again!

(She closes her eyes.)

THE END

NOTES

PLEASE SEND YOUR FEEDBACKS AT daspradip0036@gmail.com

Printed in Great Britain
by Amazon

47328461R00078